From the Pages of *Listen* (and *One Day You'll Be Giv.*

Too often, we are too arrogant to know that we have much to learn in this world. Too often, we assume that we have a grasp on things, when in actuality, we have no clue what is going on. – **CHAPTER 1**

Why is listening and receiving advice so hard for many of us? It is as if we feel insulted when we receive help or are forced to listen. It is one thing to listen advice from someone who is older than us, but to listen to advice from someone who are own age or younger than us seems unfathomable. Oftentimes, the best of us feel humble enough to receive advice and listen, improving with every encounter. – **CHAPTER 1**

Truly being open to guidance doesn't mean that you don't know the answer, it means you are humble enough to admit that there's a possibility, as slight as it could be, that you don't know the answer. Having that type of mentality is the only way to grow, because you only grow when you are tested, and in order to pass a test, you must listen. - **CHAPTER 1**

You never do know when you might receive a lesson from someone you deem less educated than yourself however high and mighty you think you are, so rather than close your ears, keep them open and you just might find that you'll advance. Call it wild, but you just might advance behind your wildest dreams. – **CHAPTER 1**

To understand someone, you've got to listen; you've got to be paying close attention to what the other is going through more than what you are going through. Environmentalists often says tread lightly and leave no trace. Understanding someone can be phrased in the opposite manner: tread heavily where they have tread, then you'll be able to make a trace on their hearts & in their lives. - **CHAPTER 2**

Being skilled will take you far, but if you get to the point where you are so skilled that you don't believe you can need aid to better yourself, you are in treacherous territory. - **CHAPTER 3**

Whether we'd like to admit it or not, we're drawn to people who listen to us. Usually the people who listen to us tend to be in a lower or similar status than us. That's why, when someone we perceive as powerful than us takes the time an effort to listen to us, we appreciate that instance more than a normal instance. God, in his mighty power, never fails to listen to us. If God never fails to listen to us, why do we constantly fail to listen to others? – **CHAPTER 3**

I realize much of my writing is of a very personal tone, especially on the subject of my fight with mental illness, but when I realized that my writing was having an impact on people in a positive way, all the embarrassment and shame went away… God gave me the ability to think, be creative, and write in order to help people whether they be Christian or not. I take great pride in being part of God's team, and it only happened because I listened to his call. – **CHAPTER 4**

Listening can be oh so difficult because of our pride. We like to think that we know it all, more often than not, and to receive advice is seen as something weak, lacking true purpose.
– CHAPTER 4

Our Lord our God tells us to live boldly, to take a risk, to surprise many including ourselves. How does one gain the capacity to surprise oneself? I've learned, that more often than not, in order to have the capacity to surprise ourselves, we must look at life as someone who is at the bottom of a swimming pool. No matter how hard we try to stay at the bottom, we seem to always come up with force. Trusting that God gave you the force to do anything seems incomprehensible is something that must always been implanted in the back of your mind. **– CHAPTER 5**

A stud's purpose is to form a vertical structural load. It can also be non load-bearing. Studs hold in place windows, doors, interior finish, exterior sheathing or siding, insulation and utilities, but, if you ask a contractor, what the most important thing a stud does is to give shape to a building. Finding a person who shapes you is the person who God wants you to be with. **– CHAPTER 6**

To be truly known by the other starts with the other listening and absorbing information to realize not only what other makes the person tick, but what moves the other person—what makes the other person not only get out of bed, but also keeps the person from going back to bed in the middle of the day.
– CHAPTER 6

Gardeners and contractors may not seem like they would at all be a similar profession, but they are both building something—something that is meant to last and be used. Both professions also require listening. Not listening in the sense of hearing but listening in the sense of knowing what their admirers or habitants want. If they're good at they're profession, their wants begin to be innate; they naturally want to build a foundation that lasts until eternity. – **CHAPTER 6**

When you think of a leader who is adaptable, you think of someone who is not only calm under pressure, but someone who is not naïve to different circumstances; they can assure their followers that no matter what, their plan will work whatever is thrown their way. – **CHAPTER 7**

When people think of arrogance, they often judge someone based on the fact if this person brags a lot. I, on the other hand, look to see if they are humble enough to admit that they in fact do not know it all. – **CHAPTER 7**

Luckily, with God's word, we have instructions on how to make every decision in life. All we have to do is listen to him and trust that even if it is the harder path, listening to His choice makes us live with purpose. – **CHAPTER 8**

I've sometimes wondered why I use so many quotations in my books from others, and, at the beginning of my books have included two or three from each chapter. I've come to the conclusion it is because, above all, people tell us quotes and share quotes with us to encourage, to inspire. – **CHAPTER 9**

Find people that challenge you. When you do this, you'll often find the challenges you face in the future are less difficult because the training this person has put you through. The weak surround themselves with people who are too timid to stick up to them, while the strong get the feeling that no future battle should be left untested. **– CHAPTER 9**

By admitting that I was not only wrong in one area of my actions but could have improved my area in another area actions, I just got a lot better. If we think about it, when someone critiques our actions, instead of our first thought being to say that they're wrong, we might ask them for additional things we need to work on because we might feel as if they are tip-toeing around us to make sure our feelings don't get hurt if they brought up additional issues. **– CHAPTER 9**

Leaders are on the unquenchable quest to get better. The best CEO's make performance reviews two-sided instead of the boss just focusing on the employee is performing. This way, the CEO gets better, and when the CEO gets better, he/she can lead more effectively. **– CHAPTER 9**

Music has a way of lifting us up in a way that nothing else quite can. It moves us, challenges us; in short, it is the both the glue and motor that binds and pushes us to pursue life in a different way we never thought was possible. We listen to music; not only to hear the instruments, but to hear the lyrics teach just as a school-teacher lectures at a podium. Will we listen to them? Are we both humble and strong enough to do just that? **– CHAPTER 10**

Age is not only the exact prerequisite for wisdom, but experience. A young person can draw from experiences just as an elder can. It doesn't happen very often, but when it does, you better being willing to listen and be humble, for one of the definitions of humble is ranking low in a hierarchy or scale. Can you make yourself low to become high? **– CHAPTER 10**

My best contributions to the world have started with listening, while my failures have often been the direct result of an ability to listen. **– CHAPTER 11**

The strong don't mind feeling as if they don't have to be in control. Control to them means controlling themselves first. From there, they feel like they have a handle on every situation that arises. **– CHAPTER 12**

Our eyes swell when are filled with emotion. The only way that can happen to us is if we feel listened to. When are listened to, feel that we are cared for, and, when we are cared for, we know are loved. **– CHAPTER 12**

You feel a void most in your life not when you cannot have the latest dress, car, or house, but when you lose something that is dear to you. This is why relationships are so much more important than things. **– CHAPTER 12**

When you receive and or give meaningful advice, a bond is formed between both individuals that can't be broken. It's as if you become on the same teams, one hand lifting up the other towards a common goal. **– CHAPTER 12**

ALSO BY THOMAS FELLOWS

Forget Self-Help
He Spoke with Authority
The Criminal
Mrs. Dubose's Last Wish

TO BE PUBLISHED IN THE FUTURE BY THOMAS FELLOWS

LISTEN UP: SEEK ENOUGH ADVICE, AND, ONE DAY, YOU'LL BE GIVING IT
ALONE AT THE LUNCH TABLE: HOW TO RISE FROM REJECTION
WHEN YOU SEE IT: BELIEF IN UNCERTAINTY
AFTER THE SHAMPOO: CONDITIONED FOR EXCELLENCE
INPUT-OUTPUT: OUR FINAL PRODUCT COMES FROM OUR INITIAL ACTIONS
RELATIVELY SPEAKING: WHEN AND WHEN NOT TO COMPARE YOURSELF TO THE REST
OVERLOOKED: BEING AND FINDING THAT DIAMOND IN THE ROUGH
ROLLING THE DICE: RISK AVERSION EXPLAINED
CONSTANT ENABLING: CREATING AN ATMOSPHERE OF PERMANENT CHANGE
SETTING PROPER EXPEXTATIONS: ALLOWING YOURSELF TO GET CAUGHT OFF GUARD LESS
LOST AND FOUND: BRING OUT THE BOX
REIN HIM IN: BE BOLD, FORGET THE LASSO

LISTEN UP
SEEK ENOUGH ADVICE, SO ONE DAY YOU'LL BE GIVING IT

THOMAS FELLOWS

Listen Up
Seek Enough Advice, So One Day You'll Be Giving It

ISBN 978-1-954617-22-3 paperback

978-1-954617-23-0 eBook

Yawn's Publishing
678-880-1922 www.yawnspublishing.com

www.yawnspublishing.com

678-880-1922
Canton, Georgia

Printed in the United States of America

CONTENTS

---

[1] Implied

Introduction

When I was walking to my favorite spot to work in Atlanta, I had an interesting thought: I'm about to start my 6th book. If you were to ask most people after that thirty to forty-five minute which ensued, how much did you write, I would have answered *nothing* because a larger part of the time I spend on books isn't just *writing*, but it could be *reading* (a book), it could be *watching* (a movie), or it could be *listening* (to a song.) Little did they know, that in order for these books to be decent at all, I had to read many books; that's why I encourage you, the reader, in the subtitle of this book, to *Seek Enough Advice, So One Day You'll Be Giving It.*

To quote another writer, David Brooks, in the introduction to his *New York Times* best-selling book, *The Second Mountain,* "when it comes to what we writers do, I like to apply an observation by D.T. Niles: "We are like beggars who try to show other beggars where we found bread. You have to get only a few pages into this book to realize that I quote a lot of people wiser than myself. I mean *a lot* of people. I'm unapologetic about this. It's occurred to me many times over the course of writing this book that maybe I'm not a writer. I'm a teacher or middle-man. I take the curriculum of other people's knowledge and I pass it along." My books are not impactful because I'm merely telling my stories;

they're impactful[2] because of all the rich sources I bring, which intertwine with the message I hope to impart on you, the reader.

*

The book is not only about practicing the art of listening to others, but also practicing the art of listening to God. Many times, we want to do things on our own, our own way, but James 1:25 says, "But whoever looks intently into the perfect law that gives freedom, and continues in it—not forgetting what they have heard, but doing it—they will be blessed in what they do." The times where I have remembered just that are times in which I have thrived the most—both for my own sake and for The Lord, but the times in which I thought I had everything figured out on my own, I have faltered.

More than anything, listening requires a caring and humble nature, caring in the sense that you have the wherewithal to forget about yourself if but for a moment and focus on someone else, and the humbleness to believe that you, in fact, do not have it all figured out. You only begin to know someone when you listen to them; we're only known to others when they not only hear us but hear us out.

Through my usual use of literature, historical figures, scripture, popular music, popular movies, and my own personal experiences, I try to not only encourage you, the reader, to not only listen to others, but listen to God's call as well. Malcom Gladwell once said, "good writing does not succeed or fail on the strength of its ability to persuade. It succeeds or fails on the strength of tis ability to engage you, to make you think, to give you a glimpse into

---

[2] At least, I hope they're impactful.

someone else's head." I hope I achieved this this throughout the pages of *Listen Up: Seek Enough Advice, So One Day You'll Be Giving It.*

Preface

Golf has been a game that has always been special to me ever since I was of a young age. Being introduced to the game by my brother Chris, and my maternal grandparents, Alan and Lynn Neal, I soon took a liking to it and it became my favorite sport, displacing basketball, baseball, and swimming. I pick two movies in this book to analyze that are both golf related: *Tin Cup* and *Happy Gilmore*. I pick these movies because in each of them there are distinct elements of the movies that illustrate the importance of listening. Both involve some sort of romance as well.

My goal growing up was to be a professional golfer. I used to dream of playing on Sunday on the tree-lined fairways of Augusta National. While I became better than average golfer in high-school[3], junior year, I completely lost my game; it was never to recover. I had a homemade swing (rarely took formal lessons) and eventually, that caught up with me. Still, I love to get out to the course whenever possible, anxious to give it my best shot.

To my knowledge, there is no other sport, which requires the amount of coaching—and therefore, listening—as the sport of golf. Additionally, there is no more scared relationship than that

---

[3] I shot 75 or better 7 times in competition. That would have gotten some looks from some small D-1 schools. I even shot 30 on nine holes in competition sophomore year.

19

of a golfer and his caddie. When someone is struggling with putting the ball, one of the first pieces of advice a caddie or coach will often give the player is to *listen* to the ball go into the hole because oftentimes, when putting, our jerk reaction is to see whether we made the putt or not. Doing this often forces the putt to go off-line because we do not stay down on the ball—causing the putt to go off-kilter. One of my best friends, who was a better golfer than me, reminded me once that God's commandments aren't to limit us; they're to make our life even fuller. I will attempt to make this exact claim throughout this book to you, the reader. Whether or not you've ever played the game enough to know that golf is a "good walk spoiled," there are parallels between life and golf that cannot be ignored.

Acknowledgements

I want to thank Luke Durham for being there for me through the years.

I want to thank Coach Gerry Romberg for encouraging in my writing the last few years.

I want to thank Winston Mayo for imparting much wisdom on me the last few years.

I want to thank Kimberly LeGrand for being a great babysitter twenty-eight years ago. It has been nice to reconnect with you!

I want to thank Jill Allen for teaching me about how the US Government operates in 5th grade.

I want to thank Suzanne Addicks for furthering my reading skills in 2nd grade.

I want to thank Elizabeth Hemphill for not giving up on me when it came to long division in 4th grade.

I want to thank Pat Engel for teaching me the preposition song in 5th grade.

I want to thank Kim Jordan for teaching me Science in 4th grade.

"It's amazing the way things, apparently disconnected, hang together." – Charlie, *Flowers for Algernon*. Daniel Keyes

When you talk, you are only repeating what you already know. But if you listen, you may learn something new. – The Dalai Lama

"So when you are listening to somebody, completely, attentively, then you are listening not only to the words, but also to the feeling of what is being conveyed, to the whole of it, not part of it." – Jiddu Krishnamurti

"A great thinker does not necessarily have to discover a master idea but has to rediscover and to affirm a true but forgotten, ignored or misunderstood master idea and interpret it in all the diverse aspects of thought not previously done, in a powerful and consistent way, despite surrounding ignorance and opposition." – Syed M. Naquib

"One of the best pieces of advice I received in my career was to 'stay curious and keep your ears to the ground.' Every single conversation requires you to turn on that listening skill and then retain what you've learned. The ability to correlate stories, remember facts and ideas that aren't your own, and then be able to share them at the right moment, can make all the difference." – Bill McDermott

To: Marzena Holly
Thanks for encouraging me to be more than
just a Buckhead Businessman

1

Two Ears, One Mouth

When I was an 8th grader at The Westminster Schools in Atlanta, GA, I had a teacher who was about as philosophical as they come. He used to tell us that if we couldn't go to sleep, to read the Bible in our beds because it would either cause us to fall asleep or we would grow in knowledge.[4] One of the phrases I remember him repeating—possibly the most often—was the phrase, "I know enough to know that I know nothing." The phrase stuck with me all of these years and still continues to be one of my favorite phrases. It's eerily similar to what Thomas Jefferson said many years ago: "he who knows best knows how little he knows."

Too often, we are too arrogant to know that we have much to learn in this world. Too often, we assume that we have a grasp on things, when in actuality we have no clue what is going on. What I've learned most from my psychiatrist that I have been recently been going to is how he responds when I give him a question. More often than not, when I do ask a question, he asks me, "what do you think?"

---

[4] In the last few years, I reminded him of this and he didn't remember saying it. At least he knew that one student was listening.

James 1:19 says, "my dear brothers and sisters, take note of this: Everyone should be quick to listen, slow to speak and slow to become angry." So many times, I find myself being the first one to talk, the first one to become angry, and, instead of being quick to listen, I am often the *last* to listen. Some advice I wish I had taken in my own life was the advice my brother and father had given me to avoid penny stocks. Doing things my own way led me to losing a great deal of money in 2014. When I look back at that mistake, in examining the mistake I made, the main determinant, which caused me to make that mistake wasn't thinking that I knew nothing, but that I knew all.

What lead to MLK Jr's impressive intelligence

I can't quote it verbatim, but if you have thirty minutes to spare, I greatly suggest you read for the first time or re-read Martin Luther King Jr.'s "Letter from Birmingham Jail." It was an open letter that King wrote in April of 1963 when he was incarcerated for participating in nonviolent demonstrations that called out the United States on its racism.

To me, what makes the letter stand out is his ability to quote past philosophers and leaders verbatim without access to the internet. If you've read this book or any of my other books, you might be impressed that I am bringing in an array of sources that I have studied in the past. It is true that I have memorized some of these quotes throughout the years, but when I write my books, I have access to the internet or to the book that I am quoting. King didn't have access to this while he was in jail, which means he literally memorized quotes from his past years to write this letter. That is quite an impressive feat. The only American I know to have had this ability would have been Abraham Lincoln. Here are some of the sources that King uses in his letter:

1. Socrates (3 times)
2. Reinhold Nieber
3. St. Thomas Aquinas
4. Shadrach, Meshach and Abednego
5. Paul of Tarsus
6. Martin Buber
7. Adolf Hitler (obviously he speaks of him in a negative light)
8. Jesus Christ
9. Amos
10. John Bunyan
11. Thomas Jefferson
12. The early Christians
13. T.S. Elliot

You see, when you use sources to back up what you say in your own writing vs. just your own opinion, you gain serious credibility with your reader. On an SAT essay where I made a perfect of 12/12, I not only quoted Thomas Jefferson, but also analyzed the racist hypocrisy of the missionary tea meetings of the ladies in Maycomb, AL in *To Kill a Mockingbird* by Harper Lee. By analyzing a quote from one of the most successful presidents of all time, and by analyzing a somewhat obscure scene from the most powerful novel of the 20th century, I proved to the graders that I could not only make an argument, but back it up in a way which showed my intelligence; after all, Daniel Kahneman is *Thinking Fast and Slow* said, "intelligence is not only the ability to reason; it also the ability to find relevant material in memory and to deploy attention when is needed." I clearly lived out this quote in my essay as did King in his letter. King's writing form, vivid metaphors, and rich language are the reason why this letter is so powerful, but I think is uncanny ability to bring is sources is even more impressive.

*

It can be a tricky situation when you need somebody to listen to you for their own good, but time and time again, they refuse to do it. Throughout *A River Runs Through It*, by Norman McClean, this is demonstrated. Below, Norman explains this predicament below:

When you are in your teens—maybe throughout your life—being three years older than your brother often makes you feel he is a boy. However, I knew already that he was going to be a master with a rod. He had those extra things besides training—genius, luck, and plenty of self-confidence. Even at his age he liked to bet on himself against anybody who would fish with him, including me, his older brother. It was sometimes funny and sometimes not so funny, to see a boy always wanting to bet on himself and almost sure to win. Although I was three years older, I did not feel old enough to bet. Betting, I assumed, was for men who wore straw hats on the backs of their heads. So I was confused and embarrassed the first couple of times he asked me if I didn't want "a small bet on the side just to make things interesting." The third time he asked me must have made me angry because he never again spoke to me about money, not even about borrowing a few dollars when he was having real money problems.

We had to be careful in dealing with each other. I often thought of him as a boy, but I could never treat him that way. He was never "my kid brother." He was a master of an art. He did not want any big brother advice or money or help, and, in the end, I could not help him.

Why is listening and receiving advice so hard for many of us? It is as if we insulted when we receive help or are forced to listen. It is one thing to listen to advice from someone who is older than us, but to listen to advice from someone who are our own age or younger than us seems unfathomable. Oftentimes, the best of us feel humble enough to receive advice and listen, improving with every encounter. David Brooks, who I mentioned in the introduction, might have put it best when he said in *The Road to Character*, "humility is the awareness that there's a lot you don't know and that a lot of what you think you know is distorted or wrong." Furthermore, in a *Harvard Business Review* article entitled, "The Art of Giving and Receiving Advice," by David A. Garvin and Joshua D. Margolis, the authors say,

When the exchange is done well, people on both sides of the table benefit. Those who are truly open to guidance (and not just looking for guidance (and not just looking for validation) develop better solutions to problems than they would have on their own. They add nuance and texture to their thinking—and, research shows, they can overcome cognitive biases, self-serving rationales, and other flaws in their logic. Those who give advice effectively wield soft influence—they shape important decisions while empowering others to act. As engaged listeners, they can also learn a lot from the problems that people being to them. And the role of reciprocity is a powerful binding force: Providing expert advice often creates an implicit debt that recipients will want to repay.

As we will learn later when I analyze the book, Paul Maclean, Norman's brother, is in desperate need for someone to help him out, but he refuses to do so because of pure arrogance. I was talking to a good friend of mine a few years back, and it seems that we can have the same attitude when we look at what Jesus Christ has done for us when he died a horrible, gruesome death. What people don't realize is that in dying that death for us, He gives our life a new purpose, a new direction & path to go forward. While God is the giver of this gift and He doesn't need anything from us, He is pleased when we live our His will and do good. Jeremiah 33:3 says, "call to me and I will answer you and tell you great and unsearchable things you do not know." That verse reminds me of what the article we just covered said when it reads,

Those who are truly open to guidance (and not just looking for validation) develop better solutions to problems than they would have on their own. They add nuance and texture to their thinking and, research shows, they can overcome cognitive biases, self-serving rationales, and other flaws in their logic.

Robert E. Lee put it quite well when he said, "the education of a man is never completed until he dies." Similarly, Thomas Jefferson once said,

When I hear another express an opinion which is not mine, I say to myself, he has a right to his opinion, as I to mine. Why should I question it? His error does me no injury, and shall I become a Don Quixote, to bring all men by force of argument to one opinion? ...Be a listener only, keep within yourself, and endeavor to establish with yourself the habit of silence, especially in politics.

Truly being open to guidance doesn't mean that you don't have the answer, it means you are humble enough to admit that there's a possibility, as potentially slight as it could be, that you don't know the answer. Having that type of mentality is the only way to grow, because you only grow when you are tested, and in order to pass a test, you must listen.

For me, I try to learn as much as possible from people whether they are deemed by society to be more "successful" than me or not. One time, I was paying for a homeless man's Subway and even asked him for advice. When most people think of the homeless, they think of us helping them, but for me, it was the other way around. In the same light, the other day, I did something that has possibly never been done in the history of mankind. I was on LinkedIn and noticed there was a fellow Westminster graduate on there, at least I thought it was a Westminster graduate. It turns out that he was still in high school and had a LinkedIn! I saw on his profile that he was senior class president, national chess master, TedX speaker, a Bible study leader, going to Stanford in the fall, and most impressive, founder of his own non-profit.

Even though he was twelve years my junior, I figured he could teach me a thing or two, and, in return, I could pay him back the favor. First, I gave him an assignment to do that I was to do myself. I told him to complete a 300-word essay in which he was supposed to explain the significance of the Rosalyn Carter quote as it related to his upcoming four years at Stanford: "You must accept that you might fail; then, if you do your best and still don't win, at least you can be satisfied that you've tried. If you don't accept failure as a possibility, you don't set high goals, you don't branch out, you don't try—you don't take the risk." I sent this to him on a Thursday afternoon at 3:11 PM expecting to get a response from him sometime that weekend, but forty-four minutes later, I got a 300-word essay from him. When you're passionate about something, the enthusiasm is impossible to be contained because what was at one time intentional becomes natural, and when something is natural to a person, it cannot be thwarted.[5]

In *Tin Cup*, Roy's crush on his new psychologist, Molly, is quote obvious. The only reason they meet in the first place is because Molly needs some advice pertaining to golf. In the opening scene, the director does a wonderful job of foreshadowing what the movie is to be about. Roy tells a riddle to his fellow employees that I told in *He Spoke with Authority* when I was describing the

---

[5] Naturally, I learned something from him. He gave me a public speaking tip that I plan on using in the future. He told me to make sure I had emphasized my opening and closing because people remember that much more than the middle.

humble nature of Bill McDermott[6] when he responded to a LinkedIn message of mine when I was only twenty-five-years-old. The riddle is below:

A man and his son are in a serious car accident. The father is killed, and the son is rushed to the emergency room. Upon arrival the attending doctor looks at the child and gasps, "This child is my son!" Who is the doctor?

Before the boys can answer, a beautiful woman walks into the room and answers, "the doctor's a woman." Soon after that, she tells Roy that she has a lesson at 7 PM. Roy looks at his calendar and asks, "I thought I had a Dr. Grisswold?" She then answers, "that's me." You never do know when you might receive a lesson from someone you deem less educated than yourself however high and mighty you think you are, so rather than close your ears, keep them open and you might find that you'll advance … call wild, but you might just advance beyond your wildest dreams.

Dreams were once what Roy had, but all he had to show for now was the being the manager of a run-down driving range in rural Texas. Molly pressed Roy on this, asking, "if you're such a legendary striker of the golf ball as everyone says, then why are you at your age out here in the middle of nowhere offering a barely solvent establishment, ducking the IRS, collecting a few pathetic dollars to buy your next 6-pack when you're capable of so much more?"

All Roy says is, "perhaps I'm chalk full of inner demons."

---

[6] Bill McDermott is former CEO of SAP and present-day CEO of ServiceNow. He has mentored me the last six years.

Molly's only response was, "perhaps you're chalk full of bull-crap."

For Molly to ask the question in the first place means that she sees potential in Roy. Very few people would knock a man while he is already down. Sometimes, I ask this same question to friends; other times I don't think it is worth it because I don't see enough potential in them. It's not easy being on the listening end of the conversations; that's for sure. But, if you can appreciate that they are asking the question because they believe in you, you're well on your way to making an impact in the world.

I know this to be true because junior year of high school at Westminster, a Dean asked this same question of me. He had a grade-wide meeting, and, a few boys, including me, acted out. I saw the Dean in the hall and he told me that of all people, he wouldn't expected me to act out. I understood him and changed my ways, acting in a better manner from then on. He happened to be the Dean who approved the decision to make the change to the dress code after I wrote a petition and got over 100 signatures of boys in the high school. Years later, when I was visiting Westminster one day, he told me something that has stuck with me. He told me that he had tried to get some boys to take similar initiatives to create change as I had but had been unable to.

*

In 1775, when George Washington took command of the Continental Army, he knew he did not have adequate knowledge and the experience in leading sizeable groups of men. To combat this this problem, and from his experience in the French and Indian War, he let his men know that, "Discipline is the soul of an army. It makes small numbers formidable; procures success to the weak and esteem to all." What is left out in the quote is that in order of this to occur and happen, his men had to trust and listen to him, just as I trusted the Dean of the boys.

Later on, Washington and his men were able to reoccupy Boston, which was important for his army because it counteracted the struggles with the Canadian campaign.

We will find out in the next chapter that Roy has the golf game to win golf tournaments with alacrity, but will he have the discipline to be successful? Will Roy *listen* to the people trying to give him aid, or will he fail to gain the wisdom necessary in order to succeed?

2

Define the Moment

Later, we're introduced to David Sims, a pro-golfer who once played college golf with Roy at Houston. Sims asks Roy to join his team for an upcoming tournament—not to play though, but to caddie for him. Through fifteen holes, Roy does his job; he gives good advice to Sims and keeps a low-profile. However, when Sims reaches the par-5 16th, Roy can't help but prove he has the most testosterone of the bunch. When Sims decides to lay up on the par-5 against David's wishes, he pokes fun at him with the fans, calling him a coward. Roy, however, hits the shot and knocks it on the green.

After the round, Romeo, who has served as Tin Cup's caddie in the past and is a fellow employee with him at the driving range, has a few words to say to Cup. First, however, Roy tells him that, "If I had it all to do over, I'd still hit that shot." He further asks Romeo, "You know why I hit that shot?" Romeo thinks it's so he could beat David Sims, but he says, "that shot was a defining moment, and when a defining moment comes along, you define the moment, or the moment defines you." Romeo then explains to him a few years back when all he needed was a twelve on a hole to join the tour, and, instead of playing the safe route and making a twelve or less, he decides to be risky and go for the gold. He ended up making a thirteen; because of his riskiness, he lost out on his dreams.

In *A River Runs Through It*, if there is any risky and bold character in the book, it is Norman's younger brother, Paul. Norman writes,

> We held in common one major theory about secret fighting—if it looks like a fight is coming, get in the first punch. We both thought that bastards aren't so tough as they talk—even bastards who look as well as talk tough. If suddenly they feel a few teeth loose, they will rub their mouths, look at the blood in their hands, and offer to buy a drink on the house. "But even if they still feel like fighting," as my brother said, "you are one big punch ahead when the fight starts."

> There is just one trouble with theory—it is only statistically true. Every once in a while you run into some guy who likes to fight as much as you do and is better at it. If you start off by loosening a few of his teeth he may try to kill you.

For Roy, that person who could kill him wasn't necessarily David Sims; it was himself. After a promising collegiate golf career, here he was in his mid-thirties, making seven dollars an hour, with no possible career trajectory, and no possible way to court a decent wife. Although he had spent his career giving advice, the last thing he needed was to give more of it; instead, he needed to *receive* advice.

It's tough to disengage from our past because it is so ingrained in us. That's why, in his concluding remarks to Congress, Lincoln said, "the dogmas of the quiet past, are inadequate to the stormy present. The occasion is piled high with difficulty, and we must rise to the occasion. As our case is new, so we must think anew, and act anew. We must disenthrall ourselves, and the we shall save our country."

Disenthralling oneself is never easy, especially when one has already made serious progress in their quest. But, in one of the most inspiring stories of the Discovery of the New World, Hernan Cortez told his men to burn their own boats in order to fulfill their mission because they were going home in their enemy's boats.[7] To achieve anything great, and, in order to be remembered, that person must with the occasion, and to do so, they should know what initially lies ahead of them are tall stairs piled high with difficulty. No one remembers the CEO whose father gave them the job, but everyone remembers the CEO who forged his own path to be at the top. This is why Roy's story could be so great, but he must listen first ...

Kind of Cute ...

Eventually, Roy does seek out advice—at least advice on how to inadvertently share his feelings with Molly, his new therapist, and ask her out. Here's the dialogue between the two after they beat around the bush for a few minutes:

---

[7] Apparently, this didn't happen, but it's still a great tale to tell...

Molly: Cut to the chase and tell me why you're here

Roy: A woman

Molly: Uh, a woman, have you asked her out?

Roy: No, she's seeing a guy, I don't know how serious it is, but the guy's a real horse's butt if you ask me

Molly: Maybe if you shared your heart with this woman, you know, took her out to dinner, it would force these issues out into the open

Roy: Well, I'm afraid she'll say no.

Molly: So what you're saying is all those speeches about swimming across shark-infested waters are really about your golf game, not about your personal life.

Roy: Well, Christ, I didn't know we were about to get into my personal life!

Molly: Well, this is therapy, Roy.

Roy: Well, I know. But I didn't think it was that type of therapy.

Molly: Well, okay, let's make this simple, Roy, please, here, sit down right here. You know these risks that you love to take on the golf course, the ones you talk so passionately and poetically about, well you need to apply those same risks to your personal life with the same passion:

Roy: You mean, I should just ask her out?

Molly: Yes

Roy: And risk, coming right over the top, snap hooking it out bounds, left.

Molly: Absolutely.

Roy: Hitting it a bit thin …

Molly: Now look, all you have to do is walk up to this woman, wherever she is, look her in the eyes, let down your guard and don't try to be cool or smooth or whatever, just to be honest and take a risk. And you know what, whatever happens, if you act from the heart, you can't make a mistake …

What happened next can be summed up by only one song: "Listen to your Heart" by Roxette. I admit I was too young to remember its release considering that was in 1988, but for some reason, I still remember how the song goes because it is such an ironic one. Per Gessle, the male half of the band, said in 1995, "This is us trying to recreate that overblown American FM-rock sound to the point where it almost becomes absurd. We really wanted to see how far we could take it." Furthermore, Gessle said that the lyrics pertained to a very good friend of Gessle who happened to be in "emotional turmoil, stuck between an old relationship and a new love. A year later, I call him up in the middle of the night after a few too many glasses of champagne, saying, "Hey, you're number one in the States."

The two words that stick out to me the most are "overblown" and "absurd." Although he was talking about sound here, actions are just as important when a man is seeking out a woman. In just the last few years, I called to make sure a girl was okay when she was sick; after which she said I was taking things too fast, I gave a card and flowers to a girl's grandmother who was friends with my grandmother only to have her cancel the date after I did so, and have had a number of letters not only returned from girls, but they never signaled if they received them. Despite the failures, I will still show girls that I care because if they don't appreciate radical empathy, how are they going to be radically empathetic with my children in the future?

Originally, when writing this book, I turned to Song of songs, which many that know the Bible well know to be the romantic section of the Bible but found myself at a loss to find anything meaningful because it seemed like every other word was beautiful. When Roy acts from the heart, he tells Molly that, "from the moment I first saw you I knew I was through with bar girls and strippers and motorcycle chicks, and when you first started talking I was smitten with you, and I'm smitten with you everyday I think about you, and the fact that you think I'm full of crap makes me even more attracted to you. Usually, I can bull crap people, but I can't bull crap you. In addition, you got great legs, and (with) most women I'm trying to think about getting in their pants from day one, but with you, I'm just thinking about how to get in your heart."

First, what Roy says reminds me of a quote from my second book, *He Spoke with Authority*, when I say, "When you're vulnerable with someone, there is a connection that cannot be broken. In laying down all your cards, you'll discover that you have the winning hand. The reason you win is by allowing the other person to see you clearly for the first time—allowing them to assist you when you need assistance, cry with you when you feel you need comfort, and help you stand when you cannot bear your own weight." You know he's being vulnerable with her because the things that he's *giving up*. Gone he says, are the bar girls and strippers; no, he says, he wants something more, something real.

Roy listens to his heart, and, in doing so, becomes a different man. Even though, when Roy asks Molly to dinner and she says no, his frankness and genuine nature changes her; she's forced into making a call to her mentor who is also a psychologist. She admits that Roy has nice green eyes and is "kind of cute." While talking, she seems to be losing her mind considering she draws circle after circle on her legal pad.

We've all been there before, thinking of a crush who completes us; or rather, that fully understand us. Understanding another person is not easy, especially if the art of understanding a person isn't practiced by one's parent or positively reinforced throughout childhood. Considering our era is now, more than ever, hypersexualized, it's amazing how little that matters to get into a girl/woman's heart. I can remember helping out with a Bible Values class senior year of high school in the elementary school at Westminster with a friend who was a girl. Without previous warning, I got all the youngsters to sign a poster for her saying thanks for coming to help out. She was shocked in a good way; I could tell it meant a lot to her.

To understand someone, you've got to listen; you've got to be paying close attention to what the other is going through more than what you are going through. Environmentalists often say tread lightly and leave no trace. Understanding someone can be phrased in the opposite manner: tread heavily where they have tread, then you'll be able to make a trace on their hearts & in their lives.

In *The Great Gatsby*, Nick Carraway, when speaking of Gatsby, says,

He smiled understandingly—much more than understandingly. It was one of those rare smiles with a quality of eternal reassurance in it, that you may come across four or five times in life. It faced—or seemed to face—the whole eternal world for an instant, and then concentrated on you with an irresistible prejudice in your favor. It understood you just as far as you wanted to be understood, believed in you as you would like to believe in yourself, and assured you that it had precisely the impression of you that, at your best, you hoped to convey.

Even a mentor of mine, Bill McGahan, took the time to send an article my way on an NBA Basketball Player, Kevin Love, who spoke to a reporter about using giving as a form of therapy during these tough times with COVID because it dovetailed perfectly with my first book, *Forget Self-Help*. We liked to be listened to; we like to be understood; because, as Gatsby says, it is rare; it may or may not happen but five times in one's life.

*

It turns out that Molly did listen to Roy. She drives to the driving range, goes up to the stairs of the RV, and comes to see Roy about to go to bed, eating what seems to be dried cereal. In possibly the most humorous scene of the movie, Molly seems to be love-struck with Roy, explaining to him in a hurried, frantic voice past failed jobs, relationships, and the sort. After a while, she even asks Roy for a stale doughnut. After she is done, she tells Roy that while she cannot see him romantically, she is willing to be his shrink to help him prepare for the US Open. It's not the complete answer that he had hoped for, but it's a start, and, considering Christianity got started with a little baby boy in a manger, sometimes a start is all you need. Listen to God for instructions. He'll tell you how to do the rest.

3

A Low-Percentage Shot

When I set out to write my first book, nobody believed in me and many from my high-school never would have expected me to write a book considering I didn't even get into my own state-school, The University of Georgia. People could stomach me having success in the sales world because I'm a personable person, but to do something as academic as writing books surprised many.

In my favorite scene of *Tin Cup*, a similar outcome is explained in the press conference following Roy's third round.

Reporter: "You, uh, went for the green on eighteen today. I'm just wondering if you think that cost you.

Roy: I saved par, didn't I?

Reporter: Well, I'm just trying to understand what you're thinking, you had the same shot yesterday on eighteen, without a head wind...

Roy: You don't think I can knock it on from there?

Reporter: Let's just say it's a low percentage shot.

Roy: Well so am I. I mean look at me, alright. I mean look at what I'm wearing, (names random small companies he's sponsored by) you think I guy like me bothers to worry about the percentages?

I had the fortune of attending one of the best college preparatory schools in the nation called The Westminster Schools in Atlanta. When I was re-reading *The Formative Years*, which describe the first twenty years at the school, which was written by William "Bill" Pressly, the founder of Westminster, I was not at all surprised to see him, in chapter two entitled "Realities," to use the George Bernard Shaw (and later Robert F. Kennedy quote) that William "Bill" McDermott[8] uses in his memoir called *Winners Dream*. The quote is, "You see things; and you say 'Why?' But I dream things that never were and say, 'Why not?'"

Ironically, when people think of reality, they automatically assume it in a negative light, when that doesn't have to be the case at all if you dare to dream likes both Bills and Roy do. Reality in itself doesn't have to be stark; it can be beautiful. But, as we mentioned in the previous chapter, you have to be bold enough to define the moment instead of letting the moment define you. Anyone can dream a dream in the middle of the night before they fall asleep, but to wake afresh and take the first steps to see it through to finish takes both skill & will.

Being skilled will take your far, but if you get the point where you think you are so skilled that you don't need to better yourself, you are in treacherous territory. In Nassir Ghaemi's *New York Times* best-seller, *A First Rate Madness: Uncovering the Links Between Mental Illness and Leadership*, he describes what David Owen calls "Hubris syndrome," which he considers a disorder of power.

---

[8] Bill McDermott is the present-day CEO of ServiceNow after serving as CEO of SAP for a decade and a half. SAP is the largest software company in the world. He has mentored me the past five years.

He has studied high-ranking leaders in international politics for many years and seems to believe that steady subjection to power forces them to be unwilling to accept disapproval of their actions, or be willing to look at an idea in a way that is different than their own. Ghaemi writes that "according to Owen, such leaders become unresponsive to opposing views, speak in the royal "we," presume the beneficial judgment of history or God, ignore public opinion, demean dissent, and rigidly hold their beliefs to the contrary."

"Normally, people and events around us prevent us from developing too many illusions about the state of the world. We hear criticism or suffer setbacks that show our approach to a particular situation is misguided, and we correct our course as best we can. But leaders often lack that useful check on their illusions. Their position gives them power to ignore negative messages, or—more than likely—they're less likely to get those messages in the first place. Yes-men abound in the corridors of power. Once leaders attain power, the world gives them less and less realistic feedback, and they're better able to exert their own power to suppress or dismiss such unhappy reactions."

Leaders Listen

It was my third summer working atop Lookout Mountain at Camp Laney in Mentone, AL. I was a fixture among the grounds, in part, because of my height. The first summer, while playing softball during counselor orientation week, I caught a fly ball with my outstretched hand. From then on, I was simply known as "Christmas Tree" or "Tree" for short.

I have also been a fan of Coca-Cola since I was a young kid. Often times, when my father had asked my sister, brother, and I to do yard work, I would sneak inside and take my proverbial "Coke break." I was also brainwashed at Westminster to think of The Coca-Cola Company as the greatest company in the world.[9] Even our water dunking on field day was called the "Dasani Dunk." While I was at a restaurant in Mentone, AL when my brother and mother were visiting, I asked for a Coke for lunch. The waitress told me all the had was Pepsi. My only response to that was, "sweet tea."

All of this to say that when I got promoted to be manager of the store at Camp Laney, I foresaw my work as training to one day work for the company. I was honored with the promotion and ready to take charge. There was only one problem with my leadership style, however: I didn't listen to the WCIT's who were working for me. At approximately 3:45 PM, all of the campers descended upon the gravel road to wait in line to have an assortment of candy, ice cream, and soft drinks to partake. As a camper, this was my favorite time of the day.

For years, WCIT's had an idea to clear out inventory by offering unpopular soft drinks and snacks in a "combo" format. This "combo" was especially popular among the smaller kids because they thought it was sort of special. Whenever anyone ordered a "combo," the WCIT's bellowed, "combo" at the top of their lungs.

As an aspiring future business owner, I was not having this. I thought the right and fair thing to do would be to give the kids

---

[9] This is due to the fact that Westminster's growth early on was spurred on by a benefactor by the name of Robert Woodruff who was president of Coca-Cola from 1923-1954.

what they *actually* wanted, not what *we* wanted to give them. One day, I told the WCIT's that a "combo" was a thing of the past. If I had only known what was to happen as result of my actions…

I soon became the most hated person at camp by both the W's and the campers. When I did roll-call at pool, instead of saying "here" to indicate they were present, campers would let me know they did not approve that I had killed the "combo." During those few days, it was not safe to walk the camp grounds. Just when I thought it couldn't get any worse, some WCIT'[10]s made t-shirts that said, "Combo Killer." Finally, I relented, and let the campers and W's have their "combos" back. I even somehow made it up to the W's by taking them to see the fabled gorge during my free time.

Alfred Brendel put it best when he said, "the word 'listen' contains the same letters and the word 'silent.'" It's challenging to sit back, shut up, and take in what the other person is saying. Often times, I find myself doing what Stephen Covey says people often do in his *The 7 Habits of Highly Effective People: Powerful Lessons in Personal Change* when he says, "most people do not listen with the intend to understand; they listen with the intent to reply." I never listened to the W's or the campers; I only replied. It was my first true experience in leadership, and I failed because I failed to listen.

If I had my mentor coaching me at age twenty-one the same way he has coached me from ages twenty-five to present, things might have ended up differently because he would have encouraged me listen; after all, from his stints at Xerox, SAP, and how he

---

[10] On of the WCIT's was the son of Tom Noonan whose story you will read about in chapter 5.

as started at ServiceNow, he has been known as the *definition* of a listener.

On the 48th floor of 10 Hudson Yards in 2017 at the SAP Innovation Space, Bill McDermott gave a talk to some young employees trying to learn from his success. In his talk, he immediately told a story from his youth, which dealt with his innate ability to listen. First, he talked about his ability to listen to customers when he owned his own delicatessen at the young age of sixteen. He told the crowd, "when you're the small one, you have to do what the big is structurally unable to do or is simply unwilling to do something because they don't have the hustle or entrepreneurial spirit." He went on further to say that there were senior citizens a block away. The senior citizens wanted delivery, and they weren't getting it from the large grocery store. So, what did McDermott do? He listened and started to deliver to senior citizens. McDermott also noticed that some blue-collar workers would show up cash-rich on Friday after they got their paycheck, and by the weekend, all the money would be gone. Thus, he started a credit system with them.

The toughest people to get into the store were the teenagers who were previously frequenting the nearby 7-11. To combat the problem, and with the help of his brother, he built a video game room and let forty kids in at a time. After a while, a teenager strode up to Bill and said, "Bill, when we want good food and to be treated right, we come to your store. When we want to steal stuff, we go to 7-11."

*

Later on in the talk, Bill would prove once again to be an effective listener. Harvey Mackay once said, "you learn when you listen. You earn when listen—not just money, but respect."

McDermott was starting to have a great deal of success as young sales director, and he figured the way things are going, he would soon be in charge of the New York territory, which he saw as a big positive because he not only thought he could grow revenue, but it would also lead to greater exposure in the company considering it was the Big Apple. His boss had other plans for him, however. He challenged him and told him to go down to Puerto Rico, where the organization had just finished dead last, coming in 64th and of 64th place.

Now, when we see leaders, many times we think of how James McGregor Burns describes leadership in his book called *Leadership:*

> Many acts heralded or bemoaned as instances of leadership—acts of oratory, manipulation, sheer self-advancement, brute coercion—are not such. Much of what commonly passes as leadership—conspicuous position-taking without followers or follow-through, posturing on various public stages, manipulation without general purpose, authoritarianism—is no more leadership than the behavior of small boy marching in front of a parade, who continue to strut along Main Street after the procession has turned down a side street toward the fairgrounds.

I've known McDermott for approximately five years. What I've come to realize most about the man is that the word *small* is not in his vocabulary not because he makes himself out to be big all the time—that he most definitely does not do—but, because of his confidence, which leads to his humility and empathy, he is not afraid to make himself feel small for the sake of others. Many people feel small when they are forced to listen; McDermott, however, does not feel that way at all. When talking about the job that McDermott was asked to take in Puerto Rico, he had a few options he could take. "There are two types of people in the world: one person has to get it just right for them: perfect job, perfect pay, perfect conditions. The other one is an all-weather athlete. They go into any set of circumstances because they are there to serve their company and they're in service to their cause."

In the interview, McDermott says something quite profound: "they were expecting me to come with the answers, and instead I came with the questions." One of the reason why they struggled, the reps told him, is that the previous manager didn't listen to their wants and desires. He was a cost-cutter, and, in that fashion, he did away with their time-honored Christmas party. Immediately, after he was told this, McDermott came through and hired the most famous salsa singer in Puerto Rico. But, there was an unspoken agreement that was signed between the two parties after he did that: the reps would have to come through for McDermott.

God leads us in the same way. Isaiah's commission is below in Isaiah 6:1-8.

In the year that King Uzziah died, I saw The Lord seated on a throne, high and exalted; and the train of His robe filled the temple. Above Him stood seraphim, each having six wings: With two wings they covered their faces, with two they covered their feet, and with two they were flying. And they were calling out to one another:

"Holy, holy, holy is the LORD of Hosts; all the earth is full of His glory."

At the sound of their voices the doorposts and thresholds shook, and the temple was filled with smoke.

Then I said:

"Woe is me,

for I am ruined,

because I am a man of unclean lips

dwelling among a people of unclean lips;

for my eyes have seen the King,

the LORD of Hosts."

Then one of the seraphim flew to me, and in his hand was A glowing coal that he had taken with tongs from the altar.

And with it he touched my mouth and said:

"Now that this has touched your lips,

Your iniquity is removed

And your sin is atoned for."

Then I heard the voice of the Lord saying:

"Whom shall I send?

Who will go for us?"

And I said:

"Here am I. Send me!"

When a leader is behind you, like The Lord was behind Isaiah, you can do anything. For a leader to be behind someone, however, they must listen. Lee Iacocca, one of the few executives ever to preside over two of the big three automakers, said in his autobiography, "I only wish I could find an institute that teaches people how to *listen* at least as much as he needs to talk. Too many people fail to realize that real communicating goes in both directions."

At my last company, this was the opposite of how I was treated, and because I was treated this way, I lost confidence in my CEO, owner, and the VP of Sales who I directly reported to. First, they hired me on, and the moment when they knew I was going to be a success and make money for them, they heaped praise upon me so I would not leave. Then, as I continued to start more deals, the praise seem to vanish before my own very eyes because they did not want to be on record by saying that they were happy by my performance. Once, I started a deal with a Fortune 50 company who happened to be a former client, and the owner told me that he fired the employee because he supposedly got lazy because he had landed that big deal and could "live off the fat of the land." Later, he contradicted what he said, and I caught him in his lie.

At the Christmas party, several employees went up to me asking what techniques I was employing because word had spread around the company that I was beyond proficient at cold calling. However, when the owner introduced me to the team, he made it seem like I wasn't doing a good job. Despite the fact that the company had been around for thirty years, it had less than twenty-five employees, which is anemic growth for a technology company. Its lack of growth is due to the fact that the owner refused to listen and when he was going to cut my commission severely, it showed that he did not lead with integrity either.

Years later, while at SAP, McDermott's focus on *being there* for his employees never wavered. He was faced with a tough decision while he was CEO. He had the choice between doing what was best for the stock price of the company and doing what was best for his employees. He knew that if he paid his employees on the commission that they were owed, the stock would take a dive as a result. He decided to do just that and while the Board had McDermott's ear for the decision, he was heard by his employees, and in *Lincoln on Leadership* by Donald Phillips, he writes that

> If modern leaders don't intuitively understand human nature as well as Lincoln did, they should at least make an attempt to learn more on the subject. After all, the most important asset a business organization has is its employees. So why not spend some time and money striving to thoroughly understand what make people tick? All leaders, in every walk of life, should make this commitment to their followers. If they don't, they may soon find that they no longer qualify as leaders due to the fact that all of their followers, in one way, have abandoned them.

Whether we'd like to admit it or not, we're drawn to people who listen to us. Usually, the people who listen to us tend to be in a lower status than us. That's why, when someone we perceive as more powerful than us take the time and effort to listen to us, we appreciate that instance even more. God, in his mighty power, never fails to listen to us. If God never fails to listen to us, why do we constantly fail to listen to others?

*

I had spoken earlier about the team of Bill McDermott who he had taken from 64th out of 64th place to 1st place out of 64th. Twenty-three years later, when Bill was the CEO of SAP, he took a trip down to Puerto Rico on business and invited the old gang to dinner. When he got to the restaurant, there was no one there. He thought to himself, "this is sad, but it has been twenty-three years." Little did he know, they were all waiting behind the curtain of the stage, all ready to surprise him. People remember if you listen; in other words, to be remembered you must listen.

In similar fashion, I'd like to think that I listened to my campers from Camp Laney. To take it a step further, I'd like to say I can prove it, because ten years later, over a hundred miles away from where I was their counselor in Alabama, I still every now and then hear a college-aged kid call me "Christmas Tree." Remember, people remember you if listen; in other words, to be remembered, you must listen.

4

Listen (Do[11]) What He Says

There is only one thing for certain you must remember to walk with God and live an intentional Christian life: God, if he truly believes in you, will challenge you to live a bold life. There is no greater example of this happening in the Bible than when God calls on Abraham to sacrifice his son, Isaac. Here is the text below: notice the subtitle to this passage reads "Abraham Tested."

Abraham Tested

Some time later God tested Abraham. He said to him, "Abraham!"
"Here I am," he replied.
Then God said, "Take your son, your only son, whom you love—Isaac—and go to the region of Moriah. Sacrifice him there as a burnt offering on a mountain I will show you."
Early the next morning Abraham got up and loaded his donkey. He took with him two of his servants and his son Isaac. When he had cut enough wood for the burnt offering, he set out for the

---

[11] Implied

place God had told him about. On the third day Abraham looked up and saw the place in the distance. He said to his servants, "Stay here with the donkey while I and the boy go over there. We will worship and then we will come back to you."

Abraham took the wood for the burnt offering and placed it on his son Isaac, and he himself carried the fire and the knife. As the two of them went on together, Isaac spoke up and said to his father Abraham, "Father?"

"Yes, my son?" Abraham replied.

"The fire and wood are here," Isaac said, "but where is the lamb for the burnt offering?"

Abraham answered, "God himself will provide the lamb for the burnt offering, my son." And the two of them went on together.

When they reached the place God had told him about, Abraham built an altar there and arranged the wood on it. He bound his son Isaac and laid him on the altar, on top of the wood. Then he reached out his hand and took the knife to slay his son. But the angel of the Lord called out to him from heaven, "Abraham! Abraham!"

"Here I am," he replied.

"Do not lay a hand on the boy," he said. "Do not do anything to him. Now I know that you fear God, because you have not withheld from me your son, your only son."

Abraham looked up and there in a thicket he saw a ram[a] caught by its horns. He went over and took the ram and sacrificed it as a burnt offering instead of his son. So Abraham called that place The Lord Will Provide. And to this day it is said, "On the mountain of the Lord it will be provided."

The angel of the Lord called to Abraham from heaven a second time and said, "I swear by myself, declares the Lord, that because you have done this and have not withheld your son, your only son, I will surely bless you and make your descendants as numerous as the stars in the sky and as the sand on the seashore. Your descendants will take possession of the cities of their enemies, and through your offspring all nations on earth will be blessed, because you have obeyed me."

Then Abraham returned to his servants, and they set off together for Beersheba. And Abraham stayed in Beersheba.

If I was ordered by God to sacrifice my son I loved very dearly, I don't know what I'd do. Do you know what *you* would do? God is our teacher, our creator, but does that mean I want to listen to him and trust in Him all of the time? Absolutely not. It is important to know however that Proverbs 3: 5-6 says, "Trust in the Lord with all your heart and lean not on your own understanding; in all your ways submit to him, and he will make your paths straight." Below, I'll break down phrases and words that make up this classic Bible verse:

Trust – Trust is vital to have in our daily lives in order to live because we can't do everything on our own. Even the most successful, independent thinkers of our day such as Steve Jobs and Bill Gates relied on and trusted other people to make both Apple and Microsoft run to its fullest degree. Bill McDermott once said, "trust is the ultimate currency." In a podcast with Bill Eades which aired in 2016, Bill McDermott went on to say,

> The first thing people do in accessing a leader is essentially (asking themselves) is this person authentic, is this person real, do I trust this person? In the end, trust is the ultimate

human currency. So, the way I live it was always to have the humility to recognize my success will be based on choosing the absolute very best people, and I often told them I choose to do what I do well often; I don't choose to do what I don't do well at all; that's what you do, so you have to show them right away that you need them and the best leaders always hire the best people.

What McDermott says is not only interesting, he also inadvertently describes the relationship that God has with us, his children. In order for us to fully enter into that relationship with God, we must feel that He is authentic; we must feel that He is real; and we must feel that we can trust Him. God chooses us because he knows we can do His work if we listen. I would probably be the *last* person you think could be an author. I have severe ADD, which would make you think that I couldn't concentrate long enough to write, and ironically enough, one of the sure-fire ways you can tell if someone is bipolar is if they have trouble finishing tasks that they start. I'm about to *finish* my sixth book by age thirty-two, and the first three have received media attention. Like McDermott, God chooses us—whom He thinks is the best—because despite whatever earthly things seem to hold us back, we can always rely on the Holy Spirit to bring us through to complete His task.

The definition of authentic is of "undisputed origin; genuine." Jesus certainly fits that description because when He came down to this earth, He performed miracles that people fathomed that no ordinary person could do, and when He rose from the dead after three days, people recognized that this must be the Christ that was prophesized many years before.

For me, when Jesus was his most authentic self was when he decided to die a gruesome, painful death so we could be set free from our sins. McDermott once said, "authenticity is in demand because it is rare." Keeping that in mind, rarely does someone sacrifice for another; this definitely doesn't happen enough. I realize much of my writing is of a very personal tone, especially on the subject of my on-going fight with mental illness, but when I realized that my writing was having an impact on people in a positive way, all the shame and embarrassment went away. Just as McDermott talked about hiring the best people and putting them to work, God gave me the ability to think, be creative, and write in order to help people whether they be Christian or not. I take great pride in being part of God's team, and it only happened because I *listened* to his call.

*

Listening can be oh so difficult because of our pride. We like to think that we know it all, more often than not, and to receive advice is seen as something weak, lacking true purpose. When we get back to *A River Runs Through It*, we can see that this tension between offering and receiving help exists between the two brothers.

Paul knew how I felt about fishing and was careful not to seem superior by offering advice, but he had watched so long that he couldn't leave me without saying something. Finally he said, "the fish are out further. Probably feaing he had put a strain on family relations, he quickly added, "just a little farther."

I reeled in my line slowly, not looking behind so as not see him. Maybe he was sorry he had spoken, but having said what he said, he had to say something more. "Instead of retrieving the line straight toward you, bring it on a diagonal from the downstream side. The diagonal will give you a more resistant base to your loop so you can put more power into your forward cast and get a little more distance."

Then he acted as if he hadn't said anything and I acted as if I hadn't heard him but as soon as he left, which was immediately, I started retrieving my line on a diagonal, and it helped. The moment I felt I was getting a little more distance I ran for a fresh hole to make a fresh start in life.

At the very end of this excerpt, it's interesting that Neal speaks to the fact that because he listens, he is able to "make a fresh start in life." In *Mediations*, by Marcus Aurelius, he tells the reader, "be not ashamed to be helped; for it thy business to do thy duty like a soldier in the assault on a town. How then, if being lame thou canst not mount up on the battlements alone, but with the help of another it is possible." Aurelius puts it perfectly in his quote: much of the time we are ashamed to receive aid in a trying time, when in fact we should always be humble enough to accept help.

Even from a Biblical perspective, Proverbs 27:17 says, "as iron sharpens iron, one man sharpens another." An interesting aspect that I noticed in *Meditations*, is, at the very beginning of the book, Aurelius is constantly thanking his teachers along the way.[12]

Abraham Lincoln, himself, when speaking of George Washington, said,

Washington is the mightiest name on earth – long since mightiest in the cause of civil liberty, still mightiest in moral reformation. On that name no eulogy is expected. It cannot be. To add brightness to the sun or glory to the name of Washington is alike impossible. Let none attempt it. In solemn awe pronounce the name, and in its naked splendor leave it shining on.

There is no greater boon in life to look up to someone in order that they might help you where they have been because you have not been there before. In golf, when putting, there is no greater advantage than to see an opponent putt on a similar line that your own putt will take. Take advantage of the fact that others have tread on a similar previous path; not to do so is like refusing to take an answer to a test you are about to take. The answers to the questions can be given to you if you are only humble to enough ask.

My Swing Feels Like an Unfolded Lawn Chair

When Roy first gets to the U.S. Open , he has a case of what—in golf—is called the shanks. For a right-handed player, this means that the ball goes dead right off what is called the hozzle of the club. It's not only demoralizing to have the shanks in golf, it can be downright dangerous as Roy finds out. When he hits shank after shank, eventually, the other players on the range, are afraid for their safety.

Because of the past and ensuing embarrassment, Roy is willing to listen to whatever his caddie, Romeo, says. First, Romeo tells Roy to take all of the change he has in his right-hand pocket and put it in his left-hand pocket. Then, he tells Roy to tie his left shoe into a double-knot. Next, he tells him to turn his hat around backwards. Finally, he tells Roy to put a tee behind his left ear. After each request that Romeo gives Roy, he shoots an incredulous look back at Romeo.

I can definitely relate to the reaction that Roy gives Romeo. If we're honest with ourselves, I think we've all looked that way towards God when He had told us something either through the Holy Spirit or through His word. We must remember, however, that we're reminded in Proverbs 1:5 that "a wise man will hear and increase in learning, and a man of understanding will acquire wise counsel."

Wise counsel is just what 1990's rock star Alanis Morisette claimed to be in her 1996 smash hit, "You learn." One music publication, *PopStasche*, reviewed the song favorably, remarking, "we're graced with the wonder of 'You learn.' It provides a break from the fiery frustration yet still proves to have soul through its repetition and humility. There it goes again with its ironic beauty and all."

When speaking of Morisette's repetition, she "recommends" for the listener to do something four times. Even when I'm told to do something (or not do something) repeatedly, I still find myself making the same mistake. Is it my self-control that's an issue, or is it that I don't trust God or the other party? Why can't I learn to do right?

What's equally interesting is that, when speaking of learning, Morisette, repeats the phrase "you learn" twenty-five times, telling the listener whether they love, lose, scream, etc., they will always learn.

Even though the main sports that I played were basketball and golf, I became a lifeguard to work at the pool for my summers at Laney. Laney often had groups up, whether they were church groups or school groups, to camp before and after the main four sessions in camp.

I was invited to be the lifeguard for a church group a few times. One time, I was invited to host The Darlington School at the river. Even though a student was only ten years old, there was a little girl who apparently had never been taught how to swim. When I found this out, it became my mission to teach her. When she got in the water, she first held on to me tightly, worried that she may drown. After a while, however, I convinced her that she would be safe now matter what, that I wouldn't let her drown. Eventually, I convinced her to hold on to me with just one arm. A strange thing happened when she realized she could somewhat swim on her own with holding on to me with one arm. Instead of becoming more scared, she became calmer, being appreciative of my strength, and more confident on her own. In short, she listened to me.

Because she had success, she continued to listen to me, and eventually let go of my arm, being able to swim on her own. Notice how in the sentence above, that I talk of her continuing to listen to me. Even if I took away the "eventually let go of my arm," it would be implied that she was able to swim on her own. In other words, just like I explain in this chapter's title, when someone listens to someone, it is implied that they did what was being told to them. If only we listened to what God tells us to do by listening to His Word and the Holy Spirit … Maybe, just maybe, we would be able to swim.

5

Break the Bones in Your Right Hand

From the outset of the final round between the antagonist and Roy, you know that this will be a competition between going for it and playing it safe. Roy tells David, "Fairways and greens David, and don't forget to wave as I blow by." David responds with, "you mean blow up, don't you sport? You always do." As the round progresses, Roy takes risk after risk, in part, because he knows, that in life, to produce anything meaningful, you do have to take risks. One of my all-time favorite stories of risk-taking involves a friend's father who founded a company called ISS. In an article in the *Georgia Tech Alumni Magazine* entitled, "On an Epic Winning Streak," Osayi Enodlyn writes, "The man has certainly never been afraid to work. An Atlanta native, Noonan grew up off of Briarcliff Road and snagged his first paper-route at the age of 8. He delivered the Atlanta Constitution, as it was known then, riding his bike—until he got a better gig at a country club when he turned 12. (It paid $1.60 an hour.) By the time Noonan got to Georgia Tech, he figured out he was wired differently than some of his classmates who were most interested in landing solid jobs with Fortune 500 companies. He converted old Coca-Cola vending machines so that they sold beer cans instead and placed them (where else?) in houses up and down frat row.

When he first started ISS, he took major risks, the boldest one being that he maxed out 37 credit cards when the company started to get going. Years later, ISS would eventually have 3,000 employees and traded on the NASDAQ.

On the second hole of the final round of the U.S. Open, Roy would have traded the position where his ball came to rest with just about anyone. When the reporter, Gary McCord, was commentating on what McAvoy must do, he simply stated the obvious: "He's in jail here, no chance for parole. In fact, the only thing he's got, he's got to hit the ball back into the fairway, try to pitch on the green, get up and down for par, he's got no chance to get on the green."

Roy's only response to his commentary was, "fifty bucks says I can knock it on the green with a seven iron." McCord's only response was, "you got it." Just as Roy had someone betting against him, Noonan, too, did in his quest to build ISS into an industry leader. While Noonan had just started to build ISS, a sizeable tech company's CEO out in Silicon Valley tried to recruit Noonan after he had served as VP of Marketing at Dun & Bradtreet. While it was a tough decision, he decided to "go for it[13] and continue to build ISS. He sent an email to the CEO informing him of this. His secretary received the reply before Noonan himself could get to it, and it said, "that's the stupidest thing I ever heard. If you get any money in that company, I'll come to Atlanta and drink champagne from a prostitute's shoe."

---

[13] More on "going for it" later.

Later on, nine months to be exact, after ISS received $3.5 million in venture capital, his secretary purchased a pair of the "gaudiest purple high-heeled shoes she could find." To say the least, one could say Noonan broke the bones in his right hand[14].

*

Taking a risk and giving it all we've got is not easy, but we can be comforted that scripture tells us in Joshua 1:9 that, "Have I not commanded you? Be strong and courageous. Do not be frightened, and do not be dismayed, for the Lord your God is with you wherever you go." Our Lord our God tells us to live boldly, to take risks, and to surprise many including ourselves. How does one gain the capacity to surprise oneself? I've learned, that more often than not, in order to have the capacity to surprise ourselves, we must look at life as someone who is at the bottom of the swimming pool. No matter how hard we try to stay at the bottom, we seem to always come up with force. Trusting that God gave you the force to do anything seems incomprehensible is something that must always have implanted in the back of your mind.

For Roy, as crazy as it seems, winning the U.S. Open was not his ultimate goal; "going for it" was much more important. Another player, Peter Jacobsen, ends up laying up because he can afford to in order to win the tournament. On the tee box at number eighteen, he says to Sims, "you ain't going to have that luxury, David. Not if you play to win."

Even though Sims was one back of Jacobsen, he decides to lay up. Roy, on the other hand, plays the role of a professor teaching Philosophy 101 at a college, and asks Romeo, his caddie, "So

---

[14] More on this later as well

this is everything, ain't it? This is the choice it comes down to. This is our immortality."

In the gallery, a friend of Molly groans, telling her, "Oh, no, this is what always happens; he's going for it. Molly, get a grip, he only needs par to tie. Tell him to lay up; he'll listen to you. You know this is why we broke up; he always went for it.

Molly's only response is, "well, my problem is that I've never been with a man who for it."

"Well, honey, he's your guy."

An announcer questions Roy, saying, "he can't get there in two, what the heck is he doing? Three days he's put the ball in the water. It will be four days if he hits this three-wood." When Roy hits the shot, everybody knows the ball is struck well enough to make it onto the green. It does end up landing on the green, however, slowly but surely the ball starts rolling back and eventually drops into the water. In golf, if you hit a shot into the water, you're allowed to drop where it last crossed the margin of the hazard, so long as it is no closer to the hole. Because of this well-known rule, everybody expected Roy to take a drop from further up the fairway and try to make a par to tie. If we've learned anything from Roy, however, he is not everybody; he wanted to make the shot that was much harder just to prove that he could do it. The announcers for CBS say a few things while he hits shot after shot into the water. Here they are below:

Jimmy, I don't believe this. He could lay up, use the drop zone, make par, force a playoff with Jacobsen, and get out of here.
What the heck is he going to do, all he had to do was walk up there and make a five for crying out loud, that's insane! Somebody tackle him!

Somebody tell this clown he doesn't have to hit it from there!

After he hits shot after shot into the water, finally, he is down to his last ball. If he loses this ball, he is disqualified from the tournament. Roy hits the shot, and not only makes it on to the green, but it ends up going into the hole for a twelve. After the round, he tells Molly, "I just gave away the U.S. Open." Molly responds with, "no one's going to remember the open: who won, who lost, but they're going to remember your twelve! It's immortal!" One better believe his explanation to the announcers who questioned his decision to go for it would be eerily similar to Mark 8:36, which says, "for what does it profit a man to gain the whole world and forfeit his soul?"

*

Later on, in *A River Runs Through It*, Norman gets the news that his brother was beaten to death because he could not pay off his gambling debts. The excerpt below describes the talk he had with his father:

> When I had finished talking with my father, he asked, "Is there anything else you can tell me?"

> Finally, I said, "nearly all the bones in his hand were broken."

> He almost reached the door and then turned back for reassurance. "Are you sure that the bones his hands were broken. "In which hand?" he asked. "In his right hand," I answered.

After my brother's death, my father never walked well again. He had to struggle to lift his feet, and, when he did get them up, they came down slightly out of control. From time to time Paul's right hand had to be reaffirmed; then my father would shuffle away again. He could not shuffle in a straight line from trying to lift his feet. Like many Scottish ministers before him, he had to derive what comfort he could from the faith that his son had died fighting.

We will often lose in life, but the real question to ask yourself when you are defeated is, "did I break the bones in my right hand?" In other words, did I leave it all out on the playing field? As I said earlier, Rosalyn Carter might have put it best when she said, "you must accept that you might fail; then, if you do your best and still don't win, at least you can be satisfied that you've tried. If you don't accept failure as a possibility, you don't set high goals, you don't branch out, you don't try—you don't take the risk." For a branch to become a branch, it must first branch away from the trunk, risking its very own survival. Many branches take that risk, knowing full well that it is not necessary. To become somebody, you have to first take that action, which is a verb in order to become a noun. Both Roy, Noonan, and Paul become a hero of sorts in their own way. Focus on the verb first, that action, and then you might just become a hero, or, that noun.

6

Hear Me Out

While I didn't vote for President Barack Obama in 2008 or 2012, there was always something that captivated me about him. It might have been the way he spoke, but the more I came to realize it, it was the way he listened. When I was in need of some inspiration one day at the Barnes & Noble on Peachtree Rd. in Buckhead, I happened to find a book that I have come appreciate in the past year. It is entitled, *To Obama: With love, joy, anger and hope.* The back cover reads, "Every night, for all eight years of his presidency, Barack Obama read and replied personally to a sampling of letters from citizens—a running dialogue with the American people. "The story of these letters is the story of a nation."

My favorite letter he responded to was a boy named Kenny Jops. He wrote:

Dear President Obama,

I heard that you are good at correcting homework. I was wondering if you would take a look at this (particularly the highlighted portion on the back.) How did I do?

Thank you,
Kenny Jops, Beaubien School
Chicago, IL

Obama responded with Kenny — Nice job on the home-work. I caught only two words misspelled on the vocabulary list.

Dream big dreams,

Barack Obama

If we dissect the first letter (that Kenny wrote), it's interesting to see that he uses the phrase, "I heard." People tend to gravitate toward people who listen, and, contrary to popular belief, the most powerful people in this world aren't the ones giving the speech, but the ones who listen first. To listen is to be humble, not thinking you know it all. In a David Brooks *New York Times* op-ed entitled "Wisdom Isn't What You Think It Is: It's More About Listening Than Talking," he writes, "When I think of the wise people in my own life, they are like that. It's not the life-altering words of wisdom that drop from their lips, it's the way they receive others. Too often the public depictions of wisdom involve remote, elderly sages who you approach with trepidation — and who give the perfect life-altering advice — Yoda, Dumbledore, Solomon. When a group of influential academics sought to define wisdom, they focused on how much knowledge a wise person had accumulated. Wisdom, they wrote, was 'an expert knowledge system concerning the fundamental pragmatics of life.'" More often than not we're moved by those type of people because they, in turn, seem to have an uncanny ability to listen and encourage us just as President Obama encourages Kenny to not only dream dreams, but dream *big* dreams.

When President Obama Could Have Listened Better

I mentioned earlier President Barack Obama's ability to listen. There was one time, however, he failed to do this. In a speech in California, he told the crowd that in April 2008 that certain people in America "cling to guns or religion." The comment was recorded by Mayhill Fowler, of Huffington Post's Off The Bus, which was an experiment in citizen journalism. Needless to say, those comments created quite a firestorm in the conservative media and even Democratic opponent Hillary Clinton seized the moment, saying, "I was taken aback by the demeaning remarks Senator Obama made about people in small-town America. His remarks are elitist and out of touch." To listen well, you've got to step outside yourself; you've got to put yourself in the other person's shoes. Obama didn't do that. To his credit, he later apologized for the comments, saying, "If I worded things in a way that made people offended, I deeply regret that." Furthermore, when we dig deeper, it seems to contradict what he said in a June 2006 speech on faith and politics when he said,

> secularists are wrong when they ask believers to leave their religion at the door before entering into the public square. Frederick Douglas, Abraham Lincoln, Williams Jennings Bryant, Dorothy Day, Martin Luther King - indeed, the majority of great reformers in American history - were not only motivated by faith, but repeatedly used religious language to argue for their cause. So to say that men and

women should not inject their "personal morality" into public policy debates is a practical absurdity. Our law is by definition a codification of morality, much of it grounded in the Judeo-Christian tradition.

I would argue that to be effective about telling someone about Christ requires more listening than talking. I was recently in Lake Charles, LA for an interview with their CBS local affiliate, and struck up a conversation with a fellow Christian at a pizza parlor. After we discussed Christianity for a while, it became apparent that we both not only appreciated our relationship with The Lord but wanted to share The Good News with others. We seemed to take a vastly different approach to doing so, however.

Here's a recent text exchange between us:

Me: Knocking on peoples doors and asking them if they are saved might not be the best way to share the Gospel; after all, how would you feel if a Muslim, Hindu, or Jew knocked on your door and told you if you didn't believe what they believed, you were going to hell?

Him: I try and be very polite.
1. "Hello, we are going around inviting people to church, do you go to church anywhere?
   A – NO
2. "More important than church, do you know what you believe it takes to go to heaven?"
3. A-No
4. "Can I show you what the Bible says it takes to go to heaven?"
5. A- No thanks

6. "May I leave you with just one verse?
7. A- Fine
8. Read Romans 10:9-10 KJV
9. Read Romans 10:9-10 KJV "That if thou shalt confess with thy mouth the Lord Jesus, and shalt believe in thine heart that God hath raised him from the dead, thou shalt be saved. 10 For with the heart man believeth unto righteousness; and with the mouth confession is made unto salvation."
10. "Would you like to hear more?"
11. A- No
12. "Thank you for your time, we are sorry for bothering you" (in sincere tone, no condescension)
13. #12. anytime someone is clearly not interested

Jesus himself listened to people. So, when trying to spread the Gospel to others, shouldn't we do the same?

*

To this day, especially in The South, gender roles are still very much traditional in many families, with the man being the breadwinner, and the woman raising the children. For me, that didn't stop me from picking two women as my role-models, one at Westminster and one at Samford. The one at Westminster was one of the few to believe that I would do great things. I've noticed that in life, the people who care about you most will both challenge and encourage you, praising you when they fell you've done a good job, and challenging you when they feel you could have done better.

The one from Westminster went to one of the very best state schools in the country and would go on to work for the top law firm in The South before deciding to teach in her mid-thirties. At Samford, I was blessed to have another teacher whom like the one from Westminster, both challenged and encouraged me. She graduated from Vanderbilt and worked in the medical device industry before she came to Samford.

When I accepted my job at a technology company after a long stint of unemployment, I didn't really know what to expect. I knew it would be different working with people in an office as I had worked the last four years in a remote setting. There was a young woman who was the closest to my age that went to a very prominent state school in The South. As we began orientation, I realized that she not only had an attractive appearance, but she was smart as a whip. One day, I overheard her tell people she was not going to be listened to on the phone because she was a dumb blond. Hours later, I texted her, strongly encouraging her to never say those words again because, in my mind, she was one of the most intelligent people I had ever run into in my life. To have a male say that, clearly the strongest salesperson in the group, and a nationally publicized author at that, meant a great deal to her, I could tell[15].

In *To Kill a Mockingbird* by Harper Lee, Atticus could tell that something was the matter with Scout when she ran outside after supper crying headfirst into their swinging bench. It seems like the most powerful people know when something is wrong with you because they are more attuned with *your* emotions rather than their

---

[15] Before you start thinking I'm a good person, I'll be the first time admit that throughout the years, I could have respected women better.

own. Anyway, Scout is crying profusely, and Atticus knows that he must be there for her. Scout explains all what went on that day. After the explanation, Atticus tells her that, "if you can learn a simple trick, Scout, you'll get along a lot better with all kinds of folks. You never really understand a person until you consider things from his point of view … until you climb into his skin and walk around in it." Scout later says, "there just didn't seem to be anyone or anything that Atticus couldn't explain."[16] Atticus, and others like Atticus, are that way because they aren't talking all of the time; they're humble and empathetic enough to look at things from your point of view. Or, they're that way because they're life-long learners; in other words, they don't think they know it all.

In the same light as Atticus was there for Scout in her time of need, Maren Morris, an up-and-coming pop star, recently explained her inspiration for her smash-hit, "The Bones." She told the interviewer, "I wrote 'The Bones' with Jim Robbins and Laura Beltz, and it was the day when I was writing in Nashville and Laura brought the title, 'The Bones,' and she always is so good at bringing stuff like that to the table, and it's always like a weird title and that's why she and I get along so well is (because) I'm willing to get weird. But she also knows how to make it so sentimental and real life and we just started talking about how gracious we were with our relationships at the time and I was really feeling so solidified with my relationship with my then fiancé, and now husband, she was feeling so amazing with her marriage and her children and Jimmy just found out that his wife was pregnant, it was like we were all super solid with our partners, and so writing this

---

[16] This is not in the actual text, but in the movie. There is a voiceover of the narrator, a fully-grown Scout, saying this.

song about the bones of a house, you know even if a hurricane comes, a storm, the wolves come, the structure of the house is still standing; the foundation is still there. So you could rip it down to the studs, and the foundation of this relationship isn't going anywhere."

In the song, you immediately know what the song is going to be about when she says, "we constructed this correctly, and because of that, it is stationary, stationary in the way you want your car to be when there is traffic coming adjacent to you." It seems like in relationships, the best way to construct them correctly, as Morris talks about, is to have open lines of communication; in other words, both parties must feel like they're being listened to by the other party. Colin Powell put it similarly when he said, "diplomacy is listening to what the other guy needs. Preserving your own position, but listening to the other guy. You have to develop relationships with other people so when the tough times comes, you can work together." In the same tone, later in the song, Morris says, "if the bones are solid, nothing else matters. The paint might shed, the glass could break, a storm could brew, but you and I remain strong together; our relationship can't collapse when the bones are strong."

Anybody's relationship can get along at a concert, on vacation, or out with friends, but what happens when the tough times truly come? To be truly known by the other starts with the other listening and absorbing information to realize not only what makes the other person tick, but what moves the other person—what makes the other person not only get out of bed, but also keeps the person from going back to bed in the middle of the day. What Morris sings about frequently during the song is about the foundation of the home. I will sometimes ask older couples what the most important part of marriage is and how to go about selecting a spouse. Recently, when I asked this question to an older lady, she simply said while you were once two, you now become one. It reminded me of something I read of Nancy Reagan when she answered young ladies questioning marriage because they were fearful of commitment.   Here's what she said below:

As far as I am concerned, I never really lived until I met Ronnie. Oh, I know that this is not the popular admission these days. You are supposed to be totally independent, perhaps having your husband around as something of a convenience. But I cannot help the way I feel.   Ronnie is my reason for being happy.

I consider Ronnie's welfare in everything I think or do. And, in return, I know I can count on him to do the right thing always in my regard. I have had 30 years now to see that he doesn't use his role of the household to dominate me in any way. He wouldn't think of acting like a dictator. You simply don't degrade someone you claim to love with mind, body, and soul.

Personal contact is important to me: the touch of my husband's hand: a tender embrace; Ronnie's coming to tell me and smiling about some good news he just cannot wait to announce. Communication. This is essential. Human beings are not islands unto themselves.

I feel sorry for young people today, this being the age of the antihero. Young people know they are missing something but cannot quite pinpoint what it is. This leads to intense frustration, a feeling that everything is wrong and nothing is right. Has my personal development been stunted by making Ronnie the focal point of my thoughts, actions, and words? Some critics may argue that I am no longer a complete, separate person but rather an extension of my husband. Yet I am reminded of the insight of the renowned French author Madame de Girardin: "To love one who loves you, to admire one who admires you, in a word, to be the idol of one's idol is exceeding the limit of human joy; it is stealing fire from heaven."

As I had mentioned earlier, I recently asked an older lady what the secret was to a successful marriage. If you remember, she said, while you were two before you got married, you are now one. It's similar to what Nancy Reagan said: "you are supposed to be totally independent, perhaps having your husband around as something of a convenience. But I cannot help the way I feel. Ronnie is my reason for being happy." When you think of a house and how it is built, there are so many things that are completely worthless until they become "one" with one another. In her interview, Morris talks about how you could rip the house down to the studs, and the foundation of the house would not go anywhere. A stud's purpose is to form a vertical structural load. It can be non-load-bearing. Studs hold in place windows, doors, interior finish, exterior sheathing or siding, insulation, and utilities, but, if you were to ask a contractor, what the most important thing a stud does the answer would to be that it gives shape to a building. Finding a person who shapes you is the person who God wants you to be with. It's not about companionship because if you focus on that you're not focusing on your outward reach to the world;

its about finding someone who makes you make the world a better place.

Strong me don't dictate; they encourage. To a select number of young women through the last few years I have sent a quote from Jane Eyre who is possibly the strongest feminist character of all time. The quote reads:

> Women are supposed to be very calm generally: but women feel just as men feel; they need exercise for their faculties, and a field for their efforts, as much as their brothers do; they suffer from too rigid a restraint, to absolute a stagnation, precisely as men would suffer; and It is narrow-minded in their more privileged fellow-creatures to say that they ought to confine themselves to making puddings and knitting stockings, to playing on the piano and embroidering bags. It is thoughtless to condemn them, or laugh at them, if they seek to do more or learn more than custom has pronounced necessary for their sex.

In my first book I use two classic works, *To Kill a Mockingbird* and *Uncle Tom's Cabin* that were written by two of the boldest women in American history: Harper Lee and Harriet Beecher Stowe. We must all believe that women weren't made to clean and cook all day. Bill McDermott certainly believes that as one of his first strategic hires at ServiceNow was a woman named Gina Mastantuono, who serves as chief financial officer, a role that is normally filled by a man.

When we get back to the last thing Nancy Reagan says, it mirrors God's relationship with his people in both the New and Old Testament. She says, "to love one who loves you, to admire one who admires you, in a word, to be the idol of one's idol. Is exceeding the limit of human joy; it is stealing fire from heaven." In the Old Testament, one of my favorite verses in Song of Songs is found in 2:3 when the beloved says, "like an apple tree among the trees of the forest is my lover among the young men. I delight to sit in his shade, and his fruit is sweet to my taste." There is love here because the beloved listens to what the lover wants, and gives it to him. Later in 2:5, the beloved says, "strengthen me with raisins, refresh with apples for I am faint of love." When we strengthen one another in relationships, we can't help but become stronger ourselves.

In The New Testament, Romans 7:4-5 says, "so, my brothers, you also die to the law through the body of Chris, that you might belong to another, to him who was raised from the dead, in order that we might bear fruit to God. For when were controlled by the sinful nature, the sinful passions aroused by the law were at work in our bodies, so that we bore fruit for death." What the two passages from both the Old and New Testament have in common is that they both speak to the power of fruit. When we think of botany, a fruit bears seeds and is formed in the ovary after flowering. A similar word to flower is *flourish*. A flower can only flourish when it is nourished first. In the same way a flower must be nourished, a foundation, too, must be built with the right materials. Gardeners and contractors may not seem like they would at all be a similar profession, but they are both building something— something that is meant to last and be used. Both professions also require listening. Not listening in the sense of hearing but listening in the sense of knowing what their admirers or habitants want. If they're good at their profession, their wants begin to be innate; they naturally want to build a foundation that lasts until eternity.

7

Every Advantage

I was talking to a friend just the other day, encouraging him to write his own book. He told me he didn't have enough life experiences to draw from and my response to that was, in order to write a book, it is more important to be well-read than have life experiences. In my opinion, authors with the most prowess are the ones who make you feel like you're reading multiple books instead of just one.

For the most part, I've always been a big reader. Only once did I use CliffsNotes throughout school, and, typically, I would read every assigned page. Eudora Welty once said that, "Indeed, learning to write may be learning how to read. For all I know, writing comes out of a superior devotion of reading.[17]

When I graduated high-school, I started to read John Grisham and brought the book along with me on Spring Break so much that a friend who was to become a fraternity brother made fun of me for it. Once I was in my mid-twenties, I began to mix

---

[17] Technically, I would read more than that because I read more of Amy Tan's *Joy Luck Club* that was assigned and read *Uncle Tom's Cabin* in entirety when a History teacher suggested that I read it, which is no small feat considering it is over 600 pages long.

in classic novels with psychology and biographies, which I've used throughout my books and in this one.

When people are impressed with my writing, it seems to them that I was born with the talent, when in actuality it has been a skill that I have had to hone the last few years. Like I said in the beginning of this book, the act of reading in the first place means that you are saying to yourself that you, in fact, do not know it all.

It's no surprise that our nation's greatest president, Abraham Lincoln, was a voracious reader. After he died, Lincoln's stepmother spoke of his love of words and what they meant ever since he was a young child: "Abe read all the books he could lay his hands on — and when he came across a passage that Struck him he would write it down on boards if he had no paper & keep it there till he did get paper — then he would re-write it — look at it repeat it — He had a copy book — a kind of scrap book in which he would put down all things and preserved them." You only preserve something when you cherish something; in other words, to cherish and preserve can be used interchangeably. The act of him writing on the boards in the first place just shows how much information he believed he could glean from reading.

Another act that proved he wanted to learn is, that at least once, he would walk several miles just to get one single book. Because he had so much knowledge stored up in his head already as president, he was able to deal with different circumstances. In fact, Harold Holzer, director of the Roosevelt House Public Policy Institute at Hunter College, has stated that, "I think Lincoln was very adaptable. I don't think Washington was. Washington did not have to operate much in the political sphere. He was contemptuous of party politics. When newspapers started attacking him in the middle of his second term, he didn't want to deal with it."

When you think of a leader who is adaptable, you think of someone who is not only calm under pressure, but someone who is not naïve to different circumstances; they can assure their followers that no matter what, their plan will work whatever is thrown their way. Lincoln, being well-read, was more readily able to decide the proper course of action more than anyone because with knowledge not only comes power, but the ability to decipher what will work and what won't work; after all, Lincoln made it a point to study history. David Brooks, again in *The Road to Character*, puts it quite nicely when he said, "We don't become better because we acquire new information. We become better because we acquire better loves. We don't become what we know. Education is a process of love formation. When you go to a school, it should offer you new things to love." If you love learning, you'll be a more successful leader because the more knowledge you have, the better you armed with making critical decisions.

Chapter nine of *Lincoln on Leadership* by Donald Phillips is entitled, "Lead by being led." True leaders don't feel that they know it all, and, because of this, they are not afraid to rely on anybody and everybody to help them out, even if that person is technically "beneath" them. Phillips writes,

> Lincoln also had the enviable quality of being able to listen to people and be guided by them without being threatened himself. He possessed the open-mindedness and flexibility necessary for worthwhile leadership. Frequently, he would listen to his subordinates' suggestions and recommendations. If they made sense, and if their course of action matched his own ideas, he would let them proceed with the knowledge and belief that it was their idea.

When people think of arrogance, they often judge someone based on if the person brags a lot. I, on the other hand, look to see if they are humble enough to admit that they in fact do not know it all. Lincoln was such a successful president because he possessed this quality.

When we think of advantages, we think of something we possess already, whether it be smarts, looks, or personality. What we often fail to consider is that we can gain these advantages by performing certain actions. There's a lot of hype right now in the media and public policy around STEM.[18] This is understandable because we need innovation in this country. We would be ignorant to come to the conclusion that studying History and English are not as important, however. The lessons that can be learned from there are just as important because how can you innovate if you don't have knowledge of the past, and those reports that you write in the labs ... don't they need to be proofread? One missed word can change the outcome of a science experiment quite a bit, can't it?

---

[18] Science, Technology, Engineering, Math

8

The Choice

Even as I sit here today, I recently had a win for both my sales career and writing career, for I just found a book that I had been looking around for many days. The book is called *Maxims of George Washington*. I have used it from time to time in my various books, which is not surprising considering one must possess wisdom to not only defeat the British Army, but also become one of the best presidents of the United States, the greatest country in the world.

How did I get started in my writing career? Well, to put it quite plainly, I simply listened. The first book doesn't happen if I didn't read *Uncle Tom's Cabin*, and I don't read *Uncle Tom's Cabin* if I didn't pay heed to the suggestion of Joe Tribble, my History teacher at Westminster. We are surrounded by people giving us advice. Some people give you advice to lift their own selves up, but many times, people are only trying to help because they care about your well-being and want you to succeed.

Thomas Jefferson, when he founded The University of Virginia, which is considered one of the top state schools in the country today, wrote in 1789, "all that is necessary for a student is access to a library."

*

In *Happy Gilmore*, a 1996 film about a crazed hockey en-
thusiast turned golfer, there is a golf pro named Chubs that wants
the best for Happy. Happy gets introduced to golf because, while
the movers are moving his grandmother's furniture out of her
home because her home is being foreclosed on due to the fact that
she hasn't paid taxes in ten years, they decide to have a long drive
contest in her front yard. When they duff a few shots, Happy
laughs, which makes one of them bet $20 that they couldn't hit a
ball longer than they did. Miraculously, Happy not only outdrives
them but ends up hitting it over 300 yards. While he doesn't like
the sport of golf, the exchange gives him the idea that he could
hustle golfers at the driving range to earn enough money to buy
back his grandmother's house.

In life, there is nothing more satisfying than for a star
performer to recognize young talent in another person that they
can mold to become the star that they have become themselves.
Chubs sees this opportunity in Happy immediately. After he sees
him drive a few balls over 300 yards, in speaking of his chances to
win the next tournament on tour, he prophetically says, "He's going to play. My God, he's going to win."

Later, in order for Happy to get ready for his upcoming
hockey season in 364 days, he decides he must spend some time in
the batting cages. He doesn't bring a bat to hit with, however, only
himself so he can be the one who gets hit by the ball in order to
toughen up.

> **Chubs:** "Come on boy, cut that out, you're making me
> sick. So you're a hockey player, huh?
> **Happy:** "Yeah."

91

Chubs: "You going to give that crap up, you're going to concentrate on golf."

Happy: "Who the heck are you?"

Chubs: "I'm the club here. Chubs Peterson. I'm offering to teach you how to play golf personally, for free."

Happy: "No."

Chubs and Happy exchange a few more words, but for Chubs, it seems impossible to convince Happy to play until Chubs challenges Happy, saying, "I thought you were primed to make the big bucks." Once Happy hears that he can't help but slam the brakes, and finally, for once, listens.

*

It seems like humans have had a long history of not listening to God, even since the beginning of time. Below describes the fall of man.

The Fall

Now the serpent was more crafty than any other beast of the field that the Lord God had made.

He said to the woman, "Did God actually say, 'You shall not eat of any tree in the garden'?" And the woman said to the serpent, "We may eat of the fruit of the trees in the garden, but God said, 'You shall not eat of the fruit of the tree that is in the midst of the garden, neither shall you touch it, lest you die.'" But the serpent said to the woman, "You will not surely die. For God knows that when you eat of it your eyes will be opened, and you will be like God, knowing good and evil." So when the woman saw that the tree was good for food, and that it was a delight to the eyes, and that the tree was to be desired to make one wise,[b] she took of its fruit and ate, and she also gave some to her husband who was with her, and he ate. Then the eyes of both were opened, and they knew that they were naked. And they sewed fig leaves together and made themselves loincloths.

And they heard the sound of the Lord God walking in the garden in the cool of the day, and the man and his wife hid themselves from the presence of the Lord God among the trees of the garden. But the Lord God called to the man and said to him, "Where are you?" And he said, "I heard the sound of you in the garden, and I was afraid, because I was naked, and I hid myself." He said, "Who told you that you were naked? Have you eaten of the tree of which I commanded you not to eat?" The man said, "The woman whom you gave to be with me, she gave me fruit of the tree, and I ate." Then the Lord God said to the woman, "What is this that you have done?" The woman said, "The serpent deceived me, and I ate."

The Lord God said to the serpent,

"Because you have done this,
cursed are you above all livestock
and above all beasts of the field;
on your belly you shall go,
and dust you shall eat
all the days of your life.
I will put enmity between you and the woman,
and between your offspring and her offspring;
he shall bruise your head,
and you shall bruise his heel."

To the woman he said,

"I will surely multiply your pain in childbearing;
in pain you shall bring forth children.
Your desire shall be contrary to your husband,
but he shall rule over you."
And to Adam he said,
"Because you have listened to the voice of your wife
and have eaten of the tree
of which I commanded you,
'You shall not eat of it,'
cursed is the ground because of you;
in pain you shall eat of it all the days of your life;
thorns and thistles it shall bring forth for you;
and you shall eat the plants of the field.
By the sweat of your face
you shall eat bread,
till you return to the ground,
for out of it you were taken;
for you are dust,
and to dust you shall return."

The man called his wife's name Eve, because she was the mother of all living. And the Lord God made for Adam and for his wife garments of skins and clothed them.

Then the Lord God said, "Behold, the man has become like one of us in knowing good and evil. Now, lest he reach out his hand and take also of the tree of life and eat, and live forever—" therefore the Lord God sent him out from the garden of Eden to work the ground from which he was taken. He drove out the man, and at the east of the garden of Eden he placed the cherubim and a flaming sword that turned every way to guard the way to the tree of life.

The reason why Eve got into trouble is because she listened to the wrong person. Instead of listening to God, she listens to the Serpent. How do we know who to listen to in life?

One way I can tell I'm listening to the right voice is seeing whether that person has anything to gain by choosing their choice they told me to make. In other words, is there a conflict of interest at play, which may influence what choice they want to make?

For God, there is no conflict of interest in regard to the choice of whether we should obey him or not. A prime example of me *not* choosing what God wanted me to do, and, instead, going down my own path, was when I drank alcohol in excess in my mid-twenties. No one benefitted from me being drunk and making a fool out of myself, especially me. If I had only listened to God, I would have made more sound decisions and not hurt all the relationships I did.

When it comes to whether or not God has a conflict of interest when He is guiding us to make this or that choice, know that God doesn't necessarily want to make you happy; instead, he wants to make you fulfilled—that you have purpose and direction in life. You know when a teacher or boss leaves for the day and doesn't give you any instructions on what to do that day? You feel miserable because you know you're not going to be productive that day.

Luckily, with God's word, we have instructions on how to make *every* decision in life. All we have to do is listen to Him and trust that even if it means taking the harder path, listening to His word makes us live with purpose.

9

Arm Yourself for Battle

The next novel we will examine is *Things Fall Apart* by Chinua Achebe. You might not have heard of it, but it as powerful as it is ironic. The book has sold at least twenty million copies and has been translated into fifty-seven languages, certainly not a bad track record. Having already told you the book is rooted in irony, you can only guess how the book is going to end considering the book's first two sentences are "Okonkwo was well-known throughout the nine villages and even beyond. His fame rested on solid personal achievement."

Set in Africa in the late 1800's, at first, it details and documents the clan's livelihood in Umofia, then, in the later half of the book, it describes the white man descending into the land of the clan. As any fiction book needs conflict, the white men create that conflict for the book. In chapter one, the narrator describes Okonkwo, saying, "he had no patience with unsuccessful men." While Okonkwo was considered one of the most successful men in the clan, later we will see how the white men took that away from him.

You've probably often heard, "The Lord giveth and The Lord taken away. This comes from Job 1:21 when, to further expand on what he says, "Naked I came from my mother's womb, and I will depart. The Lord gave and The Lord has taken away; may the name of The Lord be praised." It takes a rather strong person to admit they are nothing without the benevolence and steering of The Lord. For me, as soon as I start to have success, I let people (and myself) think that I did all of the work, and not God. There's something about success that brings us further from The Lord and something about discomfort that draws us nearer to Him.

As I've both sold and handed out books in the last three years, I have found that it is the poor that are much more enamored by my books than the rich. I've sometimes wondered why I use so many quotations in my books from others, and, at the beginning of my books have included two or three from each chapter. I've come to the conclusion it is because, above all, people tell us quotes and share quotes with us to encourage—to inspire. When I decided to embark upon writing a book at age twenty in rural Alabama, that it exactly what I hoped to do. Everyone can use some encouragement; we are all fighting our own battles.

Battles come in all shapes and sizes, and, for Happy, to make enough money for her grandmother to buy back to her house, would be the toughest battle of his life. His foe would not only be himself, but also a cheesy menace called Shooter McGavin. McGavin, known as being one of the best players on tour, doesn't take easy to the fact that Happy is starting to grab the attention of players and fans alike.

But before I mentioned Shooter, I first spoke of the first foe he would have to face: himself. Just recently, I was struggling with a problem in my own life that was not only setting me back from doing the best I could do in my own life, but at the same time, was causing me a lot of pain.

I found that I was being too critical of others. This was robbing me of not only my personal freedom, but it was causing my relationships with others to fall apart. Far too often, we take a good thing from The Lord, whether it be something in His word or something that someone else has said, and we use it for ill. For me, that was taking the Bible verse Hebrews 12: 11[19] out of context. Instead of using it to help people, I hurt others with my sharp criticism, which lead to the other person questioning why I had to hurt them this way.

How did I figure out that I was doing this? I *listened.* I've had a close relationship with a man by the name of Tom Shaffer for over 15 years now. He grew up on my street in Chastain Park in Atlanta, GA. During the family issues I struggled with, he was always on my side, but to be on my side, sometimes, it felt as if he wasn't on my side because he was challenging me. Find people that challenge you. When you do this, you'll often find the challenges you face in the future are less difficult because the training this person has put you through. The weak surround themselves with people who are too timid to stick up to them, while the strong get the feeling that no future battle should be left untested.

Just this past week I talked to Tom about some issues I was having. Having had a good talk the day before, I was surprised that he was calling me during the workday. I could obviously tell he wanted to talk. I answered the phone and we talked for a while. He encouraged me not to jump to conclusions so quickly as a had

---

[19] Hebrews 12:11 reads, "discipline is unpleasant at the time, but later on produces a harvestful of peace and righteousness by those who are trained by it."

a habit of doing. As first, it sort of caught me off guard and I got a bit defensive, but by the same day or next day, I texted him this:

I think you were right about the observation of me jumping to conclusions.

I also think I am too hard on people/expect too much of them.

I think a more appropriate response to my father when he gave me the money would have been to thank him, but asked him for more tangible support.

Lincoln was known for being a pardoner and giving people second chances. He built up a lot of people that way. I need to do more of that.

On the flip side, Robert E. Lee was known more for being a disciplinarian. I probably need to stop being that as much.

By admitting that I was not only wrong in one area of my actions but could have improved my actions in other areas, I just got a lot better. If we think about it, when someone critiques our actions, instead of our first thought being to say that they're wrong, we should ask them for additional things to work on because we might feel as if they were tip-toeing around us to make sure our feelings were hurt if they brought up additional issues.

True leaders are on the unquenchable quest to get better. The best CEO's make performance reviews two-sided instead of the boss just focusing on how the employee is performing. This way, the CEO gets better, and when the CEO gets better, the whole company improves.

For many of us, we have imposter syndrome[20][21]; who am I to lead others? Jeremiah 1:5, however, tells us to believe in ourselves because The Lord believed in us first. The passage reads, "Before I formed you in the womb I knew you; before you born I set you apart; I appointed you as a prophet to the nations." With these words alone, know that your life matters, no matter what you think or what others tell you. If you're going to play a role in God's kingdom, it's up to you to be prepared to do so. Listening to the advice others give you and seeking instead of shying away from criticism is your first step in playing a big part in God's plans he has for you.

Most politicians in Washington D.C. have it all wrong when it comes to leading. George Washington did the exact *opposite* of what they do today. Washington's style of leadership was first to listen, then to learn, then to help, only then are you able to lead. So many politicians today want to grab headlines so they can write a book to promote their run for president.

In Jarrett Jackson's recent article in *Forbes*, "Do You Know How to Listen?" he says,

Techniques like reflective listening can help. If you are regularly "re-capping" what has been said, you don't allow

---

[20] Imposter syndrome is a psychological pattern in which an individual doubts their skills, talents, or accomplishments and has a persistent internalized fear of being exposed as a "fraud".

[21] Turn to page 143 immediately to see how I tricked you into thinking I'm smarter than I really am.

yourself to miss parts of the conversation. You also show the other person that they have your full attention. That helps build trust, making them like you more and therefore more likely to work on what you both agree to. Their participation in the process gives them a voice that then encourages them to believe in what they are doing and therefore put more effort and energy toward it.

So many times, rather than re-capping what the other person is saying, I find myself wanting to interject what I thought would make a valuable addition to the conversation. Just yesterday, at a steakhouse in Houston, I met a fellow who appeared to be biracial—a mix of both black and white. We talked for a few minutes about race relations before he told me the story of his ancestry. He told me that his family came from both the Cameroon and Germany. I did not see how that was possible until he told me that an ancestor of his was from Germany, owned slaves in Mississippi, and fathered many children with a female slave. He told me to this day, his family had a reunion every two years. Sadly, he explained to me, the white members of the family in Mississippi, made it a point not to come.

Many people come up to me for advice when it comes to writing a book. The fact of the matter is that I've been moderately successful at book writing has not been by giving advice, but by seeking it.

As I quote David Brooks in the introduction to his *New York Times* best-selling book, *The Second Mountain*, "We are like beggars who try to show other beggars where we found bread. You have to get only a few pages into this book to realize that I quote a lot of people wiser than myself. I mean *a lot* of people. I'm unapologetic about this. It's occurred to me many times over the course of writing this book that maybe I'm not a writer. I'm a teacher or middle man. I take the curriculum of other people's knowledge and I pass it along." Similarly, Thomas Jefferson once said, "Books constitute capital. A library book lasts as long as a house, for hundreds of years. It is not, then, an article of mere consumption but fairly of capital, and often in the case of professional men, setting out in life, it is their only capital."

As I have written this sixth and final book, I often think of all sources that I have used along the way. When I looked up *source* in the dictionary, my two favorite synonyms are *the starting point* and *place of origin*. These sources caught my attention as something that could help. I could only be a source of help to you if I made the choice to listen to them first.

10

Arm Yourself for Battle

Usually, when somebody is getting you to listen to them, they're trying to help you. On rare occasions, however, be on your guard, because they could be trying to humiliate you. When Happy Gilmore joined an evening cocktail hour with more established professional golfers, he inadvertently irked Shooter McGavin by asking where his golf jacket was considering everyone else in the circle was donning one. Shooter tells him that he will get his at the upcoming Tour Championship that fall. Later on, he also tells him to go to the number nine green because there is a supposed rite of passage that is to place there. He even tells Happy to dress nicely.

Later on that night, Happy goes. He waits for a few minutes, then after a while, the sprinklers come on full blast, soaking him. He gets humiliated in the process, but the loveable Virgina Venit comes to his rescue, consoling him and explains to him that this prank is pulled on every new pro on tour.

The next day at the tournament, when he gets the first tee box, he doesn't realize that his playing partner, Potter, would teach him a psychology lesson.

Potter – I feel a lot of solid energy coming from you. Good, positive, aura. Great, great, it's all great.

Happy – Is it always like this, with the TV cameras, and the people, and stuff?

Gary Potter – Oh, yeah, a lot of pressure. You gotta rise above it, you gotta harvest to good energy and block out the bad. Harvest energy, block bad, feel the flow, feel it, it's circular. It's like a carousel. You pay the quarter, you get on the horse, and you go up and down and around … in a circular circle with the music, the flow, all good things.

On Happy's first swing of the day, the pressure simply gets to him. The most embarrassing thing happens to him: he misses the ball completely. He makes the situation worse by going on an explicit tirade in which he uses every curse word imaginable. When Happy finally does start to play some good golf, his celebrations are as unsettling as his tirade. We'll get to see his discipline for that later. But, for now, we'll see if Happy can listen to Potter as he struggles to get his ball in the hole while he is on the green.

Gary Potter – Happy, the ball has its own energy or life force, if you will. Its natural environment is in the hole. Why don't you send him home? His bags are packed. He has his plane ticket. Bring him to the airport. Send him home. Send him home.

What Potter is telling Happy here is exactly what God tells us in Proverbs 1:32-33: "For the waywardness of the simple will kill them, and the complacency of fools will destroy them; but

104

whoever listens to me will live in safety and be at ease, without fear of harm." So many times, when I have taken things into my own hands and did what felt "right" at the time or temporarily made me the happiest, I later felt that I not only let down God, but also let myself down. God wants us to "come home" to be with him because He knows what is best for us. Believing that your actions should be guided by His principles/Word is one of the most challenging things to think about, but it is necessary for our growth and to reach out full potential.

This makes sense because following His word has never been natural to us since the Fall of Man. Society, our friends, and family might even frown upon us for following His will. In Luke 14:25-33, Jesus says that there is clearly a cost of being a disciple:

> Large crowds were traveling with Jesus, and turning to them he said: "If anyone comes to me and does not hate father and mother, wife and children, brothers and sisters-yes, even their own life-such a person cannot be my disciple. And whoever does not carry their cross and follow me cannot be my disciple.

> "Suppose one of you wants to build a tower. Won't you first sit down and estimate the cost to see if you have enough money to complete it? For if you lay the foundation and are not able to finish it, everyone who sees it will ridicule you, saying, 'This person began to build and wasn't able to finish.'

> "Or suppose a king is about to go to war against another king. Won't he first sit down and consider whether he is

able with ten thousand men to oppose the one coming against him with twenty thousand? If he is not able, he will send a delegation while the other is still a long way off and will ask for terms of peace. In the same way, those of you who do not give up everything you have cannot be my disciples."

In today's prosperity circles, such as the teachings of Joel Osteen, you are never taught to give up anything. You're taught to indulge, and in return, God will give you both health & wealth. I can say for certain that the times in which I have sacrificed for The Lord, whether that be from a financial sense or from any other pain that I have gone through, I have felt the most fulfilled. In a much more biblically based book called *The Purpose Driven Life*, you are taught in a fundamentally different way. Here is a Bible study question and answer from a Guide from the BibleTract.org.

Is being successful and fulfilling your life's purpose the same?

"Being successful and fulfilling your life's purpose are not at all the same thing; You can reach all your personal goals, become a raving success by the worlds standard and still miss your purpose in this life." – Rick Warren

Furthermore, Matthew 16:24-25 speaks to the fact that Jesus said to His disciples: "If anyone desires to come after Me, let him deny himself, and take up his cross, and follow Me. For whoever desires to save his life will lose it, but whoever loses His life for my sake will find it.

Self-help books preach that we should not deny ourselves, the exact opposite from what Jesus says that we should do to serve the purposes of God.

Sacrifice basically means *forgetting* something, which is the title of this chapter. It is defined as an "act of giving up something valued for the sake of something else regarded as more important or worthy." Giving up something inherently means that you are replacing that something with something else.

*

When we get back to *Things Fall Apart*, the novel by Chinua Achebe, which I spoke of earlier, there is a choice that Okonkwo must make according to the customs of the clan, which he is horrified to do. In order to explain the sacrifice that Okonkwo would have to make, we must first explain who a young boy named Ikemefuna is. Okonkwo, because he was so successful, was chosen by the nine villages to carry a message of war to their enemies unless they agreed to give up a young man and a virgin to atone for the murder of a man's wife. Because their enemies were afraid, they brought him a virgin and a young boy named Ikemefuna.

Before I speak of their relationship, I must first elaborate on Okonkwo the man. Many people spoke of "brusqueness in dealing with less successful men." The narrator at one point says, "Okonkwo knew how to kill a man's spirit." Okonkwo's strong temper also led him to make one of the worst decisions of his life: he beat his wife during the Week of Peace, something that he was strongly disciplined for. Despite his hard heart and prideful ways, Okonkwo seems to be struck by Ikemefuna. The narrator says,

He was by nature a very lively boy and he gradually became popular in Okonkwo's household, especially with the children. Okonkwo's son, Nwoye, who was two years younger, became quite inseparable from him because he seemed to know everything. He could fashion out flutes from bamboo stems and even from the elephant grass. He knew the names of all the birds and could set clever traps for the little bush rodents. And he knew which trees made the strongest bows.

Even Okonkwo himself became very fond of the boy - inwardly of course. Okonkwo never showed any emotion openly, unless it be the emotion of anger. To show affection was a sign of weakness,- the only thing worth demonstrating was strength. He therefore treated Ikemefuna as he treated everybody else - with a heavy hand. But there was no doubt that he liked the boy. Sometimes when he went to big village meetings or communal ancestral feasts he allowed Ikemefuna to accompany him, like a son, carrying his stool and his goatskin bag. And, indeed, Ikemefuna called him father.

After Okonwo is forced to kill him with a machete, he is a different person. Below describes the guilt he felt.
Okonkwo did not taste any food for two days after the death of Ikemefuna. He drank palm-wine from morning till night, and his eyes were red and fierce like the eyes of a rat when it was caught by the tail and dashed against the floor. He called his son, Nwoye, to sit with him in his *obi*.

But the boy was afraid of him and slipped out of the hut as soon as he noticed him dozing.

He did not sleep at night. He tried not to think about Ikemefuna, but the more he tried the more he thought about him. Once, he got up from bed and walked about his compound. But he was so weak that his legs could hardly carry him. He felt like a drunken giant walking with the limbs of a mosquito. Now and then a cold shiver descended on his head and spread down his body.

On the third day he asked his second wife, Ekwefi, to roast plantains for him. She prepared it the way he liked with slices of oil-bean and fish.

"You have not eaten for two days," said his daughter Ezinma when she brought the food to him. "So you must finish this." She sat down and stretched her legs in front of her ....

Ezinma took the dish in one hand and the empty water bowl in the other and went back to her mother's hut. "She should have been a boy," Okonkwo said to himself again. His mind went back to Ikemefuna and he shivered. If only he could find some work to do he would be able to forget. But it was the season of rest between the harvest and the next planting season. The only work that men did at this time was covering the walls of their compound with new palm fronds. And Okonkwo had already done that. He had finished it on the very day the locusts came, when he had worked on one side of the wall and Ikemefuna and Nwoye on the other.

"When did you become a shivering old woman," Okonkwo asked himself, "you, who are known in all the nine villages for your valor in war? How can a man who has killed five men in battle fall to pieces because he has added a boy to their number? Okonkwo, you have become a woman indeed."

The interesting notion about the last comment that Okonkwo makes about himself becoming a shivering old woman is that he is dead wrong; in his intense guilt about taking part in the killing of Ikemefuna, he is sanctified. It's tough listening to our innermost thoughts that tell us we were wrong, but when we do, our world becomes a better place.

Okonkwo tries to act as if killing Ikemefuna was no big deal, but it was because Ikmefuna became a big deal to him. Earlier, the text says that Okonkwo felt like a "drunken giant." That's what we all are when we give ourselves away to sin. In a passage you probably won't hear in Joel Osteen's Lakewood Church or possibly in other mega-churches, which preach a "feel good" Christian message, Paul writes,

Dead to Sin, Alive in Christ

What shall we say, then? Shall we go on sinning so that grace may increase? By no means! We are those who have died to sin; how can we live in it any longer? Or don't you know that all of us who were baptized into Christ Jesus were baptized into his death? We were therefore buried with him through baptism into death in order that, just as Christ was raised from the dead through the glory of the Father, we too may live a new life.

For if we have been united with him in a death like his, we will certainly also be united with him in a resurrection like his. For we know that our old self was crucified with him so that the body ruled by sin might be done away with, that we should no longer be slaves to sin—because anyone who has died has been set free from sin.

Now if we died with Christ, we believe that we will also live with him. For we know that since Christ was raised from the dead, he cannot die again; death no longer has mastery over him. The death he died, he died to sin once for all; but the life he lives, he lives to God.

In the same way, count yourselves dead to sin but alive to God in Christ Jesus. Therefore do not let sin reign in your mortal body so that you obey its evil desires. Do not offer any part of yourself to sin as an instrument of wickedness, but rather offer yourselves to God as those who have been brought from death to life; and offer every part of yourself to him as an instrument of righteousness. For sin shall no longer be your master, because you are not under the law, but under grace.

Slaves to Righteousness

What then? Shall we sin because we are not under the law but under grace? By no means! Don't you know that when you offer yourselves to someone as obedient slaves, you are slaves of the one you obey—whether you are slaves to sin, which leads to death, or to obedience, which leads to righteousness? But thanks be to God that, though you used to be slaves to sin, you have come to obey from your heart the pattern of teaching that has now claimed your allegiance. You have been set free from sin and have become slaves to righteousness.

I am using an example from everyday life because of your human limitations. Just as you used to offer yourselves as slaves to impurity and to ever-increasing wickedness, so now offer yourselves as slaves to righteousness leading to holiness. When you were slaves to sin, you were free from the control of righteousness. What benefit did you reap at that time from the things you are now ashamed of? Those things result in death! But now that you have been set free from sin and have become slaves of God, the benefit you reap leads to holiness, and the result is eternal life. For the wages of sin is death, but the gift of God is eternal life in Christ Jesus our Lord.

In my life, I have found myself being a slave to sin when I forget my purpose—my reason for living. In *A River Runs Through It*, the father often tells his sons the Westminster Catechism that is, "man's chief end is to glorify God, and to enjoy Him forever." I've found that is impossible to glorify God when I am sinning; the only way I can do that is to step back and remember just what my purpose in this life is. In a January 21st, 1996 sermon preached by Tim Keller, he speaks to the power that sin has over us:

The Bible says here and God himself very personally and as we're going to see, poignantly says to a particular individual, "you don't know the power of the sin that's in your heart." It's not just that our problem is sin, the Bible says yes, one of the reasons, the main reason the world is in the condition it is in is humans sin, but it is aggravated because we won't see the power of sin; we underestimate it ... God tells us in one unbelievably vivid pregnant utterance: sin is crouching at your door ... sin by its nature looks smaller, your sin always looks smaller than it is. Sin always crouches down, it hides itself, you rationalize it, but in the midst of your very ordinary life and your ordinary feelings there is a monster.

Later on in *Things Fall Apart*, Okonkwo still feels guilty for what he has done. To him, it seems to be the monster in his life as Keller says in the above sermon. If a scab is to provide cover over a wound that we may have, so, too, does guilt if you have a close relationship with God. If you have drifted too to feel guilty, you might not even feel a thing. That's when you know your sin look far too small as Keller alludes to. Make your sin look big and you will find yourself being a bigger person.

Three Songs (Not in the Same Genre)

In the words of Albert Einstein, "I often think in music. I live my daydreams in music. I see my life in terms of music." Music has a way of lifting us up in a way that nothing else quite can. It moves us, challenges us; in short, it is both the glue and motor that binds and pushes us to pursue life in a different way than we ever thought was possible. We listen to music; not only to hear the instruments, but to hear the lyrics teach just as a school-teacher lectures at a podium. Will we listen to them? Are we both humble and strong enough to do just that?

Make Yourself Low

It might seem odd to pair a song from the 1965 smash hit movie, *The Sound of Music*, a soul song released by Bill Withers in 1972, and, lastly, a song released in 2015 by Jamaican-American electronic dance music group Major Lazer; but I have, and here's why I have done it.

First, as we examine "Sixteen Going on Seventeen," we must remember how we have gotten to this scene. The oldest Van Trapp, Liesel, is being courted by Freidrich, who later on ends up being a spy for the Germans. Before they start the duet, Friedrich teases her, saying, "We'll you're such a baby!" Liesel does what 99% of us would do if we were told such a thing: she denies it, saying, "I'm 16. What's a baby about that?" John 8:32, however, tells us good things ensue when we listen to God at all times. The verse reads, "then you will know the truth, and the truth will set you free."

I was talking to a former co-worker the other day and he spoke to me about the importance of *who* to listen to. He said he give the most respect and attention to someone who he would want to trade lives with. Furthermore, he said at the very least that if there was an area that someone was better than him in, he would listen in a more intent way, so as to grasp as much knowledge as he could. In the past six years, I have slowly gained fifty pounds. I have quite a big belly now and am not proud of it. A new co-worker of mine told me time and time again what to do to lose the weight because he had lost 100 pounds many years ago. It seems simple that I would want to trade places with this guy, but my ego was so big that I couldn't stand to listen to him. I think subconsciously I felt as if I didn't have anything to learn from him because I was much better at sales than he was.

When we get back to examine the two potential young lovers in the *Sound of Music*, we see Liesel defending herself from wanting to learn, instead of being open to a different opinion and excelling because of it. Freidrich pleads with Liesel, singing to her that, "she was completely ill-equipped to handle the onslaught of men who were going to after her." He tells her that because he has more years on her, and is more prudent, thus being able to protect her in a more advantageous way.

Just as Lisel shies away from Friedrich, I, too, often find myself shying away from God's word. When that happens, I must remember the wise words of Robert E. Lee when he said, "In all my perplexities and distresses, the Bible has never failed to give me light and strength." We listen most often when we encounter perplexities and distresses, not when we are having successes.

Ultimately, because of her distress, she later on admits that she needs someone who has more years on him and is more prudent than he. The only thing is that she is wiser than Fredriech himself. Age is not only a prerequisite for wisdom, but experience. A young person can draw from experiences just as an elder can. It doesn't happen very often, but when it does, you better be willing to listen and be humble, for one of the definitions of humble is ranking low in a hierarchy scale. Can you make yourself low to become high?

Undying Loyalty

I say in *When You See It*, originally my 4th book, "that to start a relationship—there has to be a sense of permanence that will always be there. Without that, relationships cannot form properly—or at all." When relationships have undying loyalty, you know they are of the permanent variety; or, of the variety of when the bones are good as I say in Chapter 6. What must happen in order for this to occur? Both parties must listen intently.

Now, I consider myself to be center-right politically, but at the time of the 2012 election between President Barack Obama and Senator Mitt Romney, I was even more conservative, having voted Republican at every single chance, and even one time, voted in a Democratic race for the weaker candidate in hopes of affecting the general election in a way to oust the candidate who was in a stronger position to win. I was high on Mitt Romney. My Uncle worked with him at Bain in the past and my father even mailed me a shirt to Birmingham that read "Romney-Ryan" to wear proudly on campus. I watched "The O'Reiley Factor" on Fox News every night and my best friend and I, Carson Pyles, would text each other updates on the polls quite often.

However, my perspective on him changed abruptly when I heard what Romney said behind closed doors at a fundraiser than many millionaires had attended weeks before the election. It literally made my heart sink. If you don't remember what he said, here is the text from his speech that night.

> There are 47 percent of the people who will vote for the president no matter what. All right, there are 47 percent who are with him, who are dependent upon government, who believe that they are victims, who believe the government has a responsibility to care for them, who believe that they are entitled to health care, to food, to housing, to you-name-it -- that that's an entitlement. And the government should give it to them. And they will vote for this president no matter what. ... These are people who pay no income tax. ... [M]y job is not to worry about those people. I'll never convince them they should take personal responsibility and care for their lives.

I've worked hard on my books, yes, but I also attended an elite private school for thirteen years that is better than most colleges. Even from an early age, I understood that I came from a family of means. I can remember after a middle-school Honors

Day, I had my parents turn down the radio so I could thank them for sending me to Westminster. Romney, however, acted like he earned everything despite the fact that he went to a super elite private school in Michigan called Cranbrook and didn't have to pay back student loans for college. When Obama accused him of having a silver spoon, Romney told donors, "'Oh, you were born with a silver spoon,' you know, 'You never had to earn anything,' and so forth. And, and frankly, I was born with a silver spoon, which is the greatest gift you could have, which is to get born in America. I'll tell ya, there is — 95 percent of life is set up for you if you're born in this country."

Undying loyalty means not only listening to what the other person is going through but tasting it for yourself. As a high-schooler, I volunteered for an organization called The First Tee because a man by the name of Tom Cousins, who is listed as on one of my civic Atlanta heroes on my first book, tasted what people were going through himself.

Romney, when interviewed on Fox News Sunday the following year, told Chris Wallace, "That hurt. There's no question that hurt and it did real damage to my campaign."

Leaders are supposed to *listen* to their followers. When Bill McDermott stepped down from SAP to take over the reigns at ServiceNow, he had a new profile picture taken for LinkedIn. He traded in his old suit and tie he wore at the more traditional firm and exchanged it for a black long-sleeved shirt that wasn't a traditional buttoned down. I almost didn't recognize him and told my buddy Andrew Nueberger to look at his new get-up. We both had a chuckle together at his expense. But, that's what you do to truly reach people: you become one of them and empathize with them. To begin that process, you have to listen. 1st Corinthians 9:20

states just this when Paul writes, "to the Jews I became a Jew, to win the Jews. To those under the law, I became like one under the law (though I myself am not the law), so as to win those under the law." I've been so successful at cold-calling because I act in this way. Most people who cold-call are extremely robotic, which doesn't give them the ability to *connect*. Just in the past week, I have suggested multiple books to one prospect from a Fortune 20 company, and, to another prospect from a Fortune 60 company, and article on the Jewish version of The Golden Rule.

*

Enough about politics and religion. Let's get back to the music. In "Gone, Gone, Gone," by Phillip Phillips, he gets right to the point when he tells his lover[22] "when you're down and out, I'll be at your place tonight if it necessitates assistance." To provide assistance, you have to listen to what is needed. One thing that I struggle to remember is something Ernest Hemmingway once said when he quipped, "when people talk, listen completely. Most people never listen." My best contributions in the world have started with listening, while my failures have often been the direct result of my inability to listen. When we listen, other perspectives are presented much in the same way purchasing managers are required to sift through multiple vendors instead of just one. If you just look at the first potential company that comes along, you never know if they're giving you a fair deal. You're doing the best you can for the company. In the same way, when

---

[22] In this song, he could be singing to a friend. A relationship lasts when lovers and friends are used interchangeably.

you're only listening to your own perspective, you can easily be missing out on the proper course of action.

Action is required in love, which is exactly what type of song Phillip Phillips calls, "Gone, Gone, Gone." When he revealed that the second single from his album was, "The World from the Side of the Moon," he told Yahoo Canada Music that, "it's a good little love song. Todd Clark and Derek Fuhrmann, they wrote [it] and brought it to me and I thought it was a beautiful song. The more I played it live, the more I've made it more my own and people seem to really connect with it and really enjoy it so I'm excited to see how that song's going to do."

It certainly did quite well, ranking No.1 in 8 *Billboard* charts. The song's last stanza is "when you drop like a sculpture, I'll hold you before you hit the ground." Smooth descents are the hallmark of a good airline. Once you hit the ground, however, you feel it, no matter how impressive that airline is. What if there was a way to keep yourself from feeling the landing at all? That could only happen if you didn't hit the ground. That's what happens in not only relationships with others, but also your relationship with God. He never allows that interruption to happen. In a review by Simon Clearly of musicinsideu.com, he said that Phillips did a good job with the lyrical content of the song, saying it was "the backbone, the cornerstone of true love," and going on further to say, "not many people still dare to believe this kind of love exists anymore. Even fewer believe it's possible for them to live true love. Phillips got the courage to believe, and to live, and to love." Sometimes, it's hard to believe that anyone will listen to you because everyone is usually too busy with their own problems. When you do, however, it makes you feel like the possibility of true love is in fact possible, whether that be in a friendship capacity or romantic one. It's like listening to birds in the morning while you wake up, birds that fly like good airliner, not a cheap one.

Don't Always Listen to Your Coach

"Lean On," by DJ Snake and Major Lazer, is a good dance song, and I can attest to that fact; after all, I danced to it with a rather cute girl at the 2015 Georgia Tech – Florida State football game.[23] Tech , who was having a horrendous season up to that point (2-5 and winless in the Atlantic Coast Conference), was tied with FSU who, unbeaten at 6-0, was highly ranked at #9 in the nation. It was a close game to the end, with arguably the best kicker in the nation, Robert Aguayo, set to kick a long 56-yard kick as time was set to expire. You must remember, however, that he had never missed a 4th quarter kick and Florida State had won twenty-eight straight times against ACC foes, tying a record that they achieved when they came to the league in 1992.

Since the kick was so long, Aguayo had to drive the ball at lower trajectory than normal. Georgia Tech took advantage of that and blocked the ball. At that point, if you were to hear Georgia Tech coach Paul Johnson, you would have heard him literally screaming at his players to get on the ball, instead of trying to do anything fancy and risk fumbling the ball. Apparently, Tech player Lance Austin either listened and disobeyed him, misheard him, or didn't hear him altogether because he decided to pick up the ball and run. Let's leave it the announcers to describe the rest ...

---

[23] The game was actually one of the most exciting finishes in college football history. Read on.

"Aguayo from the left hash, to remain unbeaten, and perhaps a player in the College Football Playoff, and the 29th consecutive conference win ... **BLOCKED ... STUFFED ... ERASED ...** and Georgia Tech, with an opportunity ... Austin, **STILL ON HIS FEET ... ONE MAN! YOU CAN'T BELIEVE WHAT JUST HAPPENED! WHAT A TIME TO BE ALIVE**[24]

The last Florida State player with the ability to tackle Austin was Aguayo. Ironically, just two years before, a similar play happened between Alabama and Auburn. Alabama tried to kick a long field goal and Auburn wisely positioned a player in the endzone. The next thing you know, Alabama missed it and Auburn returned it for a touchdown. After that game, someone asked Aguayo if he would have made that tackle. Here's what he said:

Reporter – "Alright, so you've seen the Davis-Davis-Davis play for Auburn against Alabama. Do you make that tackle?

Aguayo – "Yeah, yeah. When I seen that, I was like, "Oh my gosh, Carson" First of all, the kicker gets rocked, and the punter, can't make the tackle. But, it is what it is. I'm always doing tackling drills at practice, and stuff. So you know, I'm ready for that."

*

Getting back to the song, however. The song was a complete success, as it reached number two on the UK Singles

---

[24] His voice cracked when he said this in pure merriment.

Chart and got all the way up to No. 4 on the US *Billboard* Hot 100 chart. As of November 2015, Spotify named the song as the most streamed song of all time at that point. The video, which was released on March 23rd, 2015, had over 2.8 billion views up until Spring 2020. Two stars, Rihana and Nicki Minaj, were offered the vocals, albeit at a slower pace, and both of them declined the chance. Producer, Diplo of Major Lazer, said both rejection were "a blessing in disguise. MO sounds better than anybody was going to sound on that record."

The lyrics of the song are both straight-forward and to the point. Whatever Major Lazer says in the first three lines is a moot point; because, in the last line of that stanza, all she says is they paid attention to one another. To pay attention also means to listen; does it not? I was coming home from my parent's home on Halloween one night and was about to take a right turn onto a side street when I saw it was blocked off by an Atlanta police officer, so that the children didn't have to worry about the cars while they bounced from house to house in search of more candy.

I ended up getting out of the car to give the officer a book. His name was John and we talked at length. The one thing that I took away from the conversation was the story he told about Colin Powell's ability to listen in his autobiography. As I'm writing now, I hadn't seen John in quite sometime, and texted him to help me find the part in his biography on listening so I could use it in my book. Minutes after texting me, John Facetimed me while in the car. What did he have with him? The copy of the Colin Powell book!

When we discussed the book, John told me that Powell did an exceptional job of only having to hear someone tell him something once and he would often remember it. In the biography, he spoke about how much that meant to people. At the same time, it's comforting to know that God is the same way. In Jeremiah 29:12, it reads, "Then you will call on me and come and pray to me, and I will listen to you." So often people forget important things in life we tell them, but God never does.

Phone Me

If you aren't familiar with the first two songs, there's a very high percentage chance you're familiar with this last one by Bill Withers. His preliminary single off his second album, *Still Bill*, "Lean on Me" is one of the most successful songs of all time. It peaked at No.1 on both the soul singles and *Billboard* Hot 100 and was picked as the 208th song in *Rolling Stone's* ranking of "The 500 Greatest Songs of All Time." It's been so popular that it is one of nine songs to have reached the top spot on *Billboard's* Hot 100 list by two different recording artist.

The basis for the song is the strong uplifting community of Salb Fork, West Virginia where Withers grew up. Although he was excited to move out to Los Angeles, he missed it deeply. Withers grew up in a battered home in a part of town where people had little means.

When interviewed by *SongFacts* about the song, he said, "I bought a little piano and I was sitting there just running my fingers up and down the piano. In the course of doing the music, that phrase crossed my mind, so then you go back and say, "OK, I like the way that phrase, Lean on Me, sounds with this song."'

In the Bible, God is unyielding about the wealthy's insistence of the wealthy caring for the poor. If fact, below is Acts 4:32-35, which describes the believers sharing their possessions.

All the believers were one in heart and mind. No one claimed that any of their possessions was their own, but they shared everything they had. [33]With great power the apostles continued to testify to the resurrection of the LORD Jesus. And God's grace was so powerfully at work in them all [34]that there were no needy persons among them. For from time to time those who owned land or houses sold them, brought the money from the sales [35]and put it at the apostles' feet, and it was distributed to anyone who had need.

Clearly, God is telling us that we can never give to others enough. In the same vein, in the version of the song initially written by Withers, he says "you can phone me, man," he says "phone me" so many times (fourteen in total) that many radio stations, including the single version, cut the "phone me" part out due to time constraints and the repetitious nature.

Withers encourages the listener to phone him because he is willing to listen with both ears. As we will see in the next chapter, there is someone else who is powerful with the ability to listen. Because she does such a good job of it, she has others in complete heartbreak when she dies. Your heart only has the ability to be broken when you feel valued, and you only feel of value when you've been listened to.

12

Listen and Enable

When I was at the Skyland Trail mental illness rehabilitation center in the summer and fall of 2008, the song that I listened to most on my Walkman CD was, "My Stupid Mouth," by John Mayer. As human beings, I've noticed that we feel much more comfortable speaking rather than listening. Is it because we feel more in control that way?

The strong don't mind feeling as if they don't have to be in control. Control to them means controlling themselves first. From there, they feel like they have a handle on every situation that arises. One person who seems to be in control throughout the novel of *Uncle Tom's Cabin* by Harriet Beehcer Stowe is a character named Eva. Eva is only five years old but has the wisdom of Solomon and the empathetic nature of Jesus. Here are two characters describing Eva below ...

"Well, she's so loving! After all, though, she no more than Christ-like," said Miss Ophelia; "I wish I were like her. She might teach me a lesson."

"It wouldn't be the first time a little child had been used to instruct an old disciple, if it *were* so," said St. Clare.

In the same vein, in Taylor Swift's new single, "Cardigan," she repeats the phrase, "If you're in the beginning stages of life, people readily assume that you have nothing to contribute." This couldn't be further from the truth if someone were to examine Eva. I've written about 10-15 classic novels during the course of these six books and by far, she is my favorite character. She defines some lyrics in one of my favorite songs by Dave Matthews called Mercy when he sings, "caring for someone else is not timid; no, caring for others projects strength more than anything."

Eva sure did listen and care for others. The person who she most listened to was Tospy, a slave who everyone at the plantation looked at as a useless trouble-maker. That's why Topsy reacted the way she did below when Eva passed away ...

Adolph and Rosa had arranged the chamber; volatile, fickle and childish, as they generally were, they were soft-hearted and full of feeling; and, while Miss Ophelia presided over the general details of order and neatness, it was their hands that added those soft, poetic touches to the arrangements, that took from the death-room the grim and ghastly air which too often marks a New England funeral.

There were still flowers on the shelves,--all white, delicate and fragrant, with graceful, drooping leaves. Eva's little table, covered with white, bore on it her favorite vase, with a single white moss rose-bud in it. The folds of the drapery, the fall of the curtains, had been arranged and rearranged, by Adolph and Rosa, with that nicety of eye which characterizes their race. Even now, while St.

Clare stood there thinking, little Rosa tripped softly into the chamber with a basket of white flowers. She stepped back when she saw St. Clare, and stopped respectfully; but, seeing that he did not observe her, she came forward to place them around the dead. St. Clare saw her as in a dream, while she placed in the small hands a fair cape jessamine, and, with admirable taste, disposed other flowers around the couch.

The door opened again, and Topsy, her eyes swelled with crying, appeared, holding something under her apron. Rosa made a quick forbidding gesture; but she took a step into the room.

"You must go out," said Rosa, in a sharp, positive whisper; "you haven't any business here!"

"O, do let me! I brought a flower,--such a pretty one!" said Topsy, holding up a half-blown tea rose-bud. "Do let me put just one there."

"Get along!" said Rosa, more decidedly.

"Let her stay!" said St. Clare, suddenly stamping his foot. "She shall come."

Rosa suddenly retreated, and Topsy came forward and laid her offering at the feet of the corpse; then suddenly, with a wild and bitter cry, she threw herself on the floor alongside the bed, and wept, and moaned aloud.

Miss Ophelia hastened into the room, and tried to raise and silence her; but in vain.

"O, Miss Eva! oh, Miss Eva! I wish I 's dead, too,--I do!"

There was a piercing wildness in the cry; the blood flushed into St. Clare's white, marble-like face, and the first tears he had shed since Eva died stood in his eyes.

"Get up, child," said Miss Ophelia, in a softened voice; "don't cry so. Miss Eva is gone to heaven; she is an angel."

"But I can't see her!" said Topsy. "I never shall see her!" and she sobbed again.

They all stood a moment in silence.

"She said she loved me," said Topsy,-- "she did! O, dear! oh, dear! there an't nobody left now,--there an't!"

"That's true enough" said St. Clare; "but do," he said to Miss Ophelia, "see if you can't comfort the poor creature."

"I jist wish I hadn't never been born," said Topsy. "I didn't want to be born, no ways; and I don't see no use on 't."

Miss Ophelia raised her gently, but firmly, and took her from the room; but, as she did so, some tears fell from her eyes.

"Topsy, you poor child," she said, as she led her into her room, "don't give up! I can love you, though I am not like that dear little child. I hope I've learnt something of the love of Christ from her. I can love you; I do, and I'll try to help you to grow up a good Christian girl."

Miss Ophelia's voice was more than her words, and more than that were the honest tears that fell down her face. From that hour, she acquired an influence over the mind of the destitute child that she never lost.

"O, my Eva, whose little hour on earth did so much of good," thought St. Clare, "what account have I to give for my long years?"

Reactions

1. Eyes swelled
2. Wild and bitter cry
3. Piercing wildness
4. An't nobody left now

Eyes swelled – Our eyes swell when we are filled with emotion. The only way that can happen to us is if we feel listened to. When we are listened to, we feel that we are cared for, and, when we are cared for, we know we are loved.

Wild and bitter cry – Topsy let out a wild a bitter cry simply because she was thinking what life would be like without Eva in her life. The time when you feel a void most in your life is not when you cannot have the latest dress, car, or house, but when you lose something that is dear to you. This is why relationships are so much more important than things.

Just recently, a prospect involving a deal I was working on gave me some great life advice about marriage that will be much more important than whether or not the deal closes. The advice involved a certain trick he did that ensured that there was no chance that stray conversation between another woman and him could lead to anything else. He said if there was anything suspicious that was said or done, he would immediately tell his wife, which eliminated any future hard ache. In listening to his words, I now will be on the right path to making sure I do nothing wrong if I do end up getting married.

When you receive or give meaningful advice, a bond is formed between both individuals that cannot be broken. It's as if you become on the same team, one hand lifting up the other towards a common goal. Topsy never listened to anyone on the plantation until she met Eva.

When we say, "we can't believe something or someone," we usually mean it in a negative light—a light where we are disappointed or bewildered. When Topsy first met Eva, she couldn't believe someone actually listened to her and was kind to her.

It was the first word of kindness the child had ever heard in her life; and the sweet tone and manner struck strangely on the wild, rude heart, and a sparkle of something like a tear shone in the keen, round, glittering eye; but it was followed by the short laugh and habitual grin. No! the ear that has never heard anything but abuse is strangely incredulous of anything so heavenly as kindness; and Topsy only thought Eva's speech something funny and inexplicable,-- she did not believe it.

No one previously in the house, even the fellow slaves, take the time to get to know Topsy. All we know about her background is that she was raised by a spectator and didn't have a real father or mother. All of us at one point or another, even the rich and famous, have felt like this at one point or another in our lives; so, when someone finally does listen to us, the power that simple gesture has over us is extremely powerful.

Piercing wildness – We only cry with a piercing wildness when are hurt, and we are only hurt when we are in pain, pain that is usually alleviated by someone else. When that someone is taken away from us, we don't know what to do; the only thing we really know is that we miss them very dearly.

All these years, if I've remembered one phrase from *Uncle Tom's Cabin*; it was the phrase that Eva says several times when she says, "these things sink into my heart." At one point she says this after St. Clare tells the tale of how St. Clare "breaks in" a slave, by tending to his bandages and offering him, more than anything, simple comfort.

Eva had come gradually nearer and nearer to her father, as he told the story,—her small lips apart, her eyes wide and earnest with absorbing interest.

As he finished, she suddenly threw her arms around his neck, burst into tears, and sobbed convulsively.

"Eva, dear child! what is the matter?" said St. Clare, as the child's small frame trembled and shook with the violence of her feelings. "This child," he added, "ought not to hear any of this kind of thing,—she's nervous."

"No, papa, I'm not nervous," said Eva, controlling herself, suddenly, with a strength of resolution singular in such a child. "I'm not nervous, but these things *sink into my heart.*"

"What do you mean, Eva?"

"I can't tell you, papa. I think a great many thoughts. Perhaps some day I shall tell you."

"Well, think away, dear,—only don't cry and worry your papa," said St. Clare. "Look here,—see what a beautiful peach I have got for you!"

Eva took it, and smiled, though there was still a nervous twitching about the corners of her mouth.

In order to be an impact to others, you have to have been impacted by others first; in other words, others will be touched by you only if you've been touched by others yourself. When Eva died, there was a piercing wildness in Topsy's cry because Eva cried for her first. Martin Luther King once said, "whatever affects one directly, affects all directly." In the many ways, Eva would never allow herself to become her full person until she helped Topsy become her full person first. In several lines above, I use that same word, *first*, when I explain that Eva cried for Topsy first. It reminds me of the words found in Matthew 20:16 when it reads, "So the last shall be first, and the first last; for many are called, but few are chosen." Those who become first in God's eyes have an innate ability to listen. They put their own needs last and the needs of others ahead of their own. The first step in doing this is to listen.

She felt, too, for those fond, faithful servants, to whom she was as daylight and sunshine. Children do not usually generalize; but Eva was an uncommonly mature child, and the things that she had witnessed of the evils of the system under which they were living had fallen, one by one, into the depths of her thoughtful, pondering heart. She had vague longings to do something for them,—to bless and save not only them, but all in their condition,—longings that contrasted sadly with the feebleness of her little frame.

"Uncle Tom," she said, one day, when she was reading to her friend, "I can understand why Jesus *wanted* to die for us."

"Why, Miss Eva?"

"Because I've felt so, too."

"What is it, Miss Eva?—I don't understand."

"I can't tell you; but, when I saw those poor creatures on the boat, you know, when you came up and I,—some had lost their mothers, and some their husbands, and some mothers cried for their little children,—and when I heard about poor Prue,—oh, wasn't that dreadful!—and a great many other times, I've felt that I would be glad to die, if my dying could stop all this misery. I *would die* for them, Tom, if I could," said the child, earnestly, laying her little thin hand on his.

Tom looked at the child with awe; and when she, hearing her father's voice, glided away, he wiped his eyes many times, as he looked after her.

"It's jest no use tryin' to keep Miss Eva here," he said to Mammy, whom he met a moment after. "She's got the Lord's mark in her forehead."

"Ah, yes, yes," said Mammy, raising her hands; "I've allers said so. She wasn't never like a child that's to live—there was allers something deep in her eyes. I've told Missis so, many the time; it's a comin' true,—we all sees it,—dear, little, blessed lamb!"

When we go back to my 4th book written, *When You See It: Belief in the Uncertainty*, we see the word *substitute* come back again. Eva explains that Jesus did not only die for us, He *wanted* to because he loves us that much. She explains to Tom that she was impacted by seeing the poor creatures in the slave trade. She later says that she would literally *die* for them, just so they would have some comfort.

Eva is part of the reason why I wrote my first book, *Forget Self-Help*. While I had friends from college and high-school that led the "Christan life" by having a "quiet time," refraining from getting drunk, saving sex for marriage and refraining from cussing, I never truly saw Christ in them, and because I couldn't see Christ is them, I could never *feel* Christ in them. Just recently, I talked to one of these types of Christians and he failed to be able to comfort me when I was suicidal; in fact, when I called him, he told me I should probably talk to someone else[25] Did he live as Christ would have wanted them to live? Absolutely not.

Later, when Mammy, a slave at the plantation speaks of Eva, she says she has "The Lord's mark on her forehead." She had this mark on her forehead because, better than anyone else, she listened.

Speaking of listening, Eva was never one to tell people to listen to her, but she had to because there were too many sobs and groans to talk over ...

"I sent for you all, my dear friends," said Eva, "because I love you. I love you all; and I have something to say to you, which I want you always to remember. . . . I am going to leave you. In a few more weeks you will see me no more--"
Here the child was interrupted by bursts of groans, sobs, and lamentations, which broke from all present, and in which her slender voice was lost entirely. She waited a moment, and then, speaking in a tone that checked the sobs of all, she said,
"If you love me, you must not interrupt me so. Listen to what I say. I want to speak to you about your souls. . . . Many of you, I am afraid, are very careless. You are thinking only about this

---

[25] He's very active in a ministry in Atlanta that fits the description of the previous sentences.

world. I want you to remember that there is a beautiful world, where Jesus is. I am going there, and you can go there. It is for you, as much as me. But, if you want to go there, you must not live idle, careless, thoughtless lives. You must be Christians. You must remember that each one of you can become angels, and be angels forever. . . . If you want to be Christians, Jesus will help you. You must pray to him; you must read--"

The child checked herself, looked piteously at them, and said, sorrowfully,

"O dear! you _can't_ read--poor souls!" and she hid her face in the pillow and sobbed, while many a smothered sob from those she was addressing, who were kneeling on the floor, aroused her.

"Never mind," she said, raising her face and smiling brightly through her tears, "I have prayed for you; and I know Jesus will help you, even if you can't read. Try all to do the best you can; pray every day; ask Him to help you, and get the Bible read to you whenever you can; and I think I shall see you all in heaven."

"Amen," was the murmured response from the lips of Tom and Mammy, and some of the elder ones, who belonged to the Methodist church. The younger and more thoughtless ones, for the time completely overcome, were sobbing, with their heads bowed upon their knees.

"I know," said Eva, "you all love me."

"Yes; oh, yes! indeed we do! Lord bless her!" was the involuntary answer of all.

"Yes, I know you do! There isn't one of you that hasn't always been very kind to me; and I want to give you something that, when you look at, you shall always remember me, I'm going to give all of you a curl of my hair; and, when you look at it, think that I loved you and am gone to heaven, and that I want to see you all there."

It is impossible to describe the scene, as, with tears and sobs, they gathered round the little creature, and took from her hands what seemed to them a last mark of her love. They fell on their knees; they sobbed, and prayed, and kissed the hem of her garment; and the elder ones poured forth words of endearment, mingled in prayers and blessings, after the manner of their susceptible race.

Dear – When we say someone is dear, we mean that we value them. Don't you feel valued when someone actually listens to you? I sure do because it shocks me for the *rights* reasons, instead of the *wrong* reasons.

Interrupted – How do you get to the point where you're interrupted by groans and sobs during one of your last talks with a a group of people before you're about to die? You can only achieve this by proving that you listened to them in the first place. Without you, they feel like no one will ever be there to listen to them, thus enabling to do their very best. Fitting it, isn't it? That we end this chapter with the title of it. *Listen and enable.* A friend and mentor once taught me that phrase. I'll never forget it, for I wanted to be counted on to do it, thus changing lives and changing my own in the same pivotal sweep.

13

Come on, Let's Go

When we get back to Happy Gilmore, we see a man desperate for change in his golf game, so desperate that he asks Chubbs to give him a second chance and agrees to have help him out again. Chubbs wants to know that he's serious about getting better before actually taking him up on the offer.

To convince him, he tells Chubbs, "I'm stupid. You're smart. I was wrong. You were right. You're the best. I'm the worst. You're very good looking. I'm not attractive."

"Alright, as long as you're willing to admit that now. Are you ready to get down to business and do exactly what I'm going to tell you to do?"

You would expect that Happy and Chubbs would start their lessons at a golf course. If you thought that, however, you would be wrong. Of all places, they go to a miniature golf course, the type of course you would play at on vacations.

Immediately, when Happy gets to the miniature golf course, he says, "this is embarrassing; I'm a professional golfer, for God's sake."

Chubbs fires back with, "No, it's your short game that's embarrassing. Come on, let's go.

*

After a while, Happy and Chubbs finally get to the final hole where the clown's mouth is blocking every ball that Happy putts and at it, spitting it back out at Happy. We've all been there in life. Whatever we do, we can't seem to get moving, to get to our final destination. What Chubbs does next is what God tells us to do when we are struggling: we need to get to our "happy place."

For me, this means when I am going through a tough time, I need to remember what is most important in life. Obviously, all of us have to make a living, but at the end of the day, our goal should be to live the earth a better place than how we found it. When Abraham Lincoln was considering committing suicide, he told his friend Joshua Speed, "I have an irrepressible desire to live 'till I can be assured the world is a little better for my having lived in it." In the same light, for the most part, the work that I do in technology sales is a very mundane task. Thirty to forty percent of my work is called "prospecting," a task where I look up on LinkedIn and Discover.Org, contacts to cold call. It is quite tedious and calling people isn't much better. It is also a mundane, thankless task.

But if I do make serious money, the most encouraging thing to me is what I'm going to do with that money. Immediately when I first got to Houston, I noticed there was a serious problem with homelessness and beggars; they seemed to be at every corner I ran down. I immediately thought of the work that my mentor Bill McGahan did when he founded Georgia Works. According to their website, the organization transforms chronically homeless men into self-sufficient and productive members of society. It also develops and implements cost-effective, comprehensive programs that meet the needs of a diverse population working to break the cycles of homelessness, addiction and criminal recidivism.

Ultimately, because Happy[26] and my "happy place" isn't about us, we end up working harder because there is a larger purpose in mind. When I was unemployed for a year, I know how awful I felt & I don't want anyone to have to go through that.

I don't want vs. *I don't want anyone* – When we add an "anyone" to the end of the phrase "I don't want," the phrase sounds much different; it sounds much more about others than ourselves. That can only happen through listening, however, because if we don't listen to other's needs and desires in the first place, we can never deliver them.

*

Of all the controversial topics discussed in my books, none may be as controversial than talk about the one I'm about to talk about: colonization. Chinua Achebe, author of the book we have examined, *Things Fall Apart*, once said, "until the lions have their own historians, the history of the hunt will always glorify the hunter."

While I endorse The Great Commission of Matthew 28:19-20, many colonialists were not doing what they were doing to spread Christianity, they were doing it for money, power, and control. The most despicable treatment the native Africans got is outlined in the article, "Tradition and Modernity in Chinua Achebe's *African Trilogy*" by Jago Morrison.

---

[26] If you can remember, Happy wanted to make the money to get his grandmother back in her own house that her husband built.

In part three of *Things Fall Apart* Achebe suggests this very clearly when he introduces the District Commissioner's regime. The new dispensation is framed, from the start, as simultaneously inescapable and characterized by remoteness and ignorance. The first we hear of the kotma, native officials of the colonial courts, is the community's hatred of them for their high-handedness and disregard of traditional obligations. When the titled men of Umuofia are arrested following the burning of Mr. Smith's church, Achebe shows them as problematically insubordinate to colonial authority too. Disobeying the instructions to respect the Umofians as titled me, they shave their heads, beat them and taunt them where they sit handcuffed, forced to urinate in their clothes. Extortion starts right away, as they exploit the language barrier between the British and the men of Umuofia.

One can only imagine the pain that the men of Umuofia must have been facing when this happened to them. Messing with a man is one thing, but to totally denigrate a man's culture and way of life is like a hot iron entering a house made of fifty year old wood.

*

While I believe that all lives matter in the United States because we are all made in the image of God, I totally understand why the Black Lives Matter Movement got started. One reason I feel this way is because of an article I read on CNN.com entitled, "Black kids go missing at a higher rate than white kids. Here's why

141

we don't hear about them" by Harmeet Kaur. In the article, she states that,

a 2010 study found that black children were significantly underrepresented in TV news. Even though about a third of all missing children in the FBI's database were black, they only made up about 20 percent of the missing children cases covered in the news.

Later in the article, she states that, "a 2015 study was bleaker: though black children account for about 35% of missing children cases in the FBI's database, they amounted to only 7% of media references."

The Black Lives Matter program got started because black people felt like they were forgotten. In the case of the disproportionately media coverage in terms of missing black children vs. white children, they clearly have a case. For whatever reason, I have always gotten along well with African-Americans[27]. The way the District Commissioner treated Okonkwo and the others reminds me of a story I was told by the former Sheriff in Houston I spoke of earlier who had ancestors from Cameroon and Germany. He told me about a story in the 1990's when he stopped at a diner out in the country town of Texas. It was 5 PM, and he was already looking for a good meal. When he went into the diner, everybody left immediately. It's a shame that just twenty-five years ago that racism still existed.

When Okonkwo returns to his homeland after his exile, he is astonished to see what his clan has become because of the white

---

[27] Honestly, I get along well with all people generally speaking.

man. Obierika, an elder in Okonkwo's land, eventually tells him that,

the white man is very clever, He came quietly and peaceably with his religion. We were amused at his foolishness and allowed him to stay. Now he has won over our brothers, and our clan can no longer act like one. He has put a knife on the things that held us together and we have fallen apart.

Later, when Obierka, Okonkwo, and others meet to decide what to do about what they must do to save their clan, a messenger from the District Commissioner interrupts them to tell them the meeting must stop at once. Okonkwo's isn't having it. He draws out his machete and kills the man. In the end, he end up killing himself. Below is the excerpt from the book of what happens next. What the District Commissioner names the book he plan on writing is pure irony.

*

Then they came to the tree from which Okonkwo's body was dangling, and they stopped dead.

"Perhaps your men can help us bring him down and bury him," said Obierika. "We have sent for strangers from another village to do it for us, but they may be a long time coming."

The District Commissioner changed instantaneously. The resolute administrator in him gave way to the student of primitive customs.

"Why can't you take him down yourselves?" he asked.

"It is against our custom," said one of the men. "It is an abomination for a man to take his own life. It is an offense against the Earth, and a man who commits it will not be buried by his clansmen. His body is evil, and only strangers may touch it. That is why we ask your people to bring him down, because you are strangers."

"Will you bury him like any other man?" asked the Commissioner.

"We cannot bury him. Only strangers can. We shall pay your men to do it. When he has been buried we will then do our duty by him. We shall make sacrifices to cleanse the desecrated land."

Obierika, who had been gazing steadily at his friend's dangling body, turned suddenly to the District Commissioner and said ferociously: "That man was one of the greatest men in Umuofia. You drove him to kill himself; and now he will be buried like a dog...." He could not say any more. His voice trembled and choked his words.

"Shut up!" shouted one of the messengers, quite unnecessarily.

"Take down the body," the Commissioner ordered his chief messenger, "and bring it and all these people to the court."

"Yes, sah," the messenger said, saluting.

The Commissioner went away, taking three or four of the soldiers with him. In the many years in which he had toiled to bring civilization to different parts of Africa he had learned a number of things. One of them was that a District Commissioner must never attend to such undignified details as cutting a hanged man from the tree. Such attention would give the natives a poor opinion of him. In the book which he planned to write he would stress that point. As he walked back to the court he thought about that book. Every day brought him some new material. The story of this man who had killed a messenger and hanged himself would make interesting reading. One could almost write a whole chapter on him. Perhaps not a whole chapter but a reasonable paragraph, at any rate. There was so much else to include, and one must be firm in cutting out details. He had already chosen the title of the book, after much thought: The Pacification of the Primitive Tribes of the Lower Niger.

Choked His Words

What's amazing to me is that Okonkwo goes from leader of his clan, to someone they refuse to bury because he committed suicide. I can only imagine the emotion with which Oberika spoke with. Achebe does a beautiful job when he describes Obierka choking his words.

When does this happen to us in our own lives? It happens when are not listened to. Just recently, I sent an email out to the company who fired me after a week even though I had been the fastest to start deals in company history. Things didn't work out because I never interviewed with the hiring manager, instead I in-

145

terviewed with the founders who loved me because they knew I would produce and make money for them. I got fired because the VP of Sales who never interviewed me felt threatened I would take his job.[28] I sent an email explaining my success that was happening at my current company, but more importantly explained what their actions had on my mental health. You see, from 2008-2019, while I struggled with depression, I had never experienced mania, which I was proud of. Taking my medication everyday and keeping myself in check led to this. After I got fired, no one communicated with me, even the person who hired me. Because of this, I got even more stressed out. Part of the exertion helped me land my next job by giving me more than ample energy to cold call several companies, but it came at a price. Looking back, I was coherent enough to see some signs of hypomania, which is the milder form of mania. Held unchecked, it can have disastrous consequences. The reason why this troubled me so much is that if I ever ran for anything in the future, it would be my duty to potential voters to disclose that this happened. In an era where there is much stigma surrounding mental illness, I knew that disclosing this could hurt my chances at being elected.

The tone of the District Commissioner tells me that he is not a man who listens well. He doesn't treat the natives as made in the image of God, even though they are pedaling Christianity. This is extremely hypocritical. I've never told Bill McDermott or Nick Tzitzon this, but when I interviewed for the job at SAP when I was twenty-five, the interviewer seemed perturbed to talk to me. (I honestly don't blame him, for I was extremely unqualified for in-

---

[28] I didn't think of this on my own. Nick Tzitzon, who has been McDermott's right hand man the last eight years, told me this may have been what happened.

terviewing for a leadership position with no substantial deals under my belt.) Eventually, in an annoyed voice, he asked if I had emailed McDermott out of the blue, which told me that I was not the only person who had tried to send him a cold-email, asking him for a job. It seems that McDermott consistently took the time and energy to not only respond to these cold-emails, but get him/her in touch with a recruiter.

Although I didn't get the job, years later it sunk into me how neat it was that he responded to my email. A CEO of a company with 75,000 employees miraculously got back to me off a cold email. I was no longer a Cunnigham[29]. All because he took the time and care to listen to me.

---

[29] See page 96 in my first book, *Forget Self-Help*, to understand that reference.

Appendix A

When you read the following paragraphs, specifically with the footnote under *imposter syndrome,* you may think that I am a really smart guy for knowing such a concept and incorporating it into this book. But if we delve deeper into my inclusion of the phrase, we see that I am really not that smart, but really just an exceptional listener. I was first introduced to the notion that someone could be an impostor by a former neighbor of mine. I hadn't seen her in a while, so I explained that I had proven people wrong who hadn't believed in me in the past. She didn't seem to grasp what I said because over and over again she kept telling me that she felt like an impostor coming out of college, meaning that people over-estimated her and she didn't believe in herself. Even after I told her this was the *opposite* of how I felt, she continued bring up her feeling like an impostor ad nauseum. She clearly wasn't *listening* to what I had to say; she couldn't put herself in my shoes. Most people after that encounter, would intentionally block that experience from than brain, thinking that there wasn't anything to learn from. I'm not like most people, though; I remembered what she said. Three months later, I was at a Barnes in Noble in Baton Rouge, LA after an interview for my fourth book. While I was charging my phone, I struck up a conversation with someone sitting down as well. We talked for a while, each exchanging advice and things that we learned. At the time, I was the most publicized

Christian author in the nation and hottest up and coming non-fiction author under 45 at age 31. I shouldn't have been taking seriously what a fitness instructor was saying about philosophical arguments, but I did. In doing so, I lived out the words of my 3rd book when I say, "to take learning even further, one has to learn from anybody and everybody, even the flawed. In doing so, your life will be changed, and once your life is changed, you will change others." I'll be the first one to say that I'm not that smart of a guy, but I'll also be the first one to say that I'm an above average listener. What I learned from him by the way was the phrase *imposter syndrome*. When you read the above excerpt, you probably thought I was smart to include it, when I really just regurgitated information from people who most people wouldn't have been listening to had they been in my position. But if you take the position that you can learn from anyone, you can trick people into thinking you're smarter than you really are.

Author's Note

In the same way that David Brooks wrote *The Road to Character* in order to "save his soul," I, too, came to the realization throughout writing this book that I need to do a better job of focusing the conversation less on myself and more on the other person. Apologies to anyone in the past when I spoke too much about myself. I would like to hope that I am not that same person today.

I realize it is a bit controversial including quotes from Thomas Jefferson considering he fathered several children with a slave of his named Sally Hemmings. I am by no means condoning his behavior by including him in this book. Jefferson, like many other Southerners, including Robert E. Lee was in favor of gradual emancipation (whatever that means.)

@ Justin Bieber: I see you have come out with *yet another* hit. "Stay" is a pretty good song, but not as good as my books. I have to admit, though; it's pretty darn catchy.

References

Chapter 1

1. "Jefferson Quotes and Family Letters." Extract from Thomas Jefferson's Batture Pamphlet, *The Proceedings of the Government of the United States, in Maintaining the Public Right to the Beach of the Mississippi, adjacet to New-Orleans, against the Intrusion of Edward Livingston, prepared for the use of Counsel.* [25 Feb. 1812]. https://tjrs.monticello.org/letter/282 .Retrieved 7-30-21.
2. James 1:19. *Holy Bible* (New International Version) Zondervan. Grand Rapids, Michigan. 1986. Page 1881.
3. *Letter From Birmingham Jail.* Martin Luther King Jr. Penguin UK. 2018.
4. *Thinking Fast and Slow.* Daniel Kahneman. Farrar, Straus and Giroux. New York. 2011. Page 46.
5. *A River Runs Through It and Other Stories.* Norman Maclean. 2017. The University of Chicago. Chicago, IL. Page 6.
6. *The Road to Character.* David Brooks. Random House. New York. 2015. Page 8 and 9.
7. "The Art of Giving an Receiving Advice." David A. Garvin and Joshua D. Margolis. January-February 2015. https://hbr.org/2015/01/the-art-of-giving-and-receiving-advice. Retrieved 7-30-21.
8. Jeremiah 33:3. *Holy Bible.* Page 1231.

9. "Robert E. Lee." https://www.biography.com/military-figure/robert-e-lee. Retrieved 7-30-21.

10. "Thomas Jefferson to Thomas Jefferson Randolph, November 24, 1808, from The Works of Thomas Jefferson in Twelve Volumes. Federal Edition. Collected and Edited by Paul Leicester Ford." November 24, 1808. http://lcweb2.loc.gov/service/mss/mtj/mtj1/042/042_1046_1049.pdf. Retrieved 7-30-21.

11. "First Ladies Influence and Image: Rosalynn Carter."http://firstladies.c-span.org/FirstLady/41/Rosalynn-Carter.aspx. Retrieved 7-30-21.

12. Quotes. https://www.quotes.net/movies/tin_cup_11675. Retrieved 7-30-21.

13. "Washington takes command of Continental Army in 1775." U.S. Army Center of Military History. April 15, 2016. US Army. https://www.army.mil/article/40819/washington_takes_command_of_continental_army_in_1775. Retrieved 7-31-21.

14. General George Washington, Instructions to Company Captains (July 29, 1757) in 4 THE PAPERS OF GEORGE WASHINGTON, Nov. 1756—Oct. 1757 341, 344 (W.W. Abbot & Dorothy Twohig eds., 1984).

Chapter 2

1. Quotes. https://www.quotes.net/movies/tin_cup_11675. Retrieved 7-31-21.

2. Maclean. Page 218.

3. "Annual Message to Congress – Concluding Remarks." Abraham Lincoln Online – Speeches and Writings. December 1st, 1862. http://www.abrahamlincolnonline.org/lincoln/speeches/congress.htm. Retrieved 7-31-21.

4. Reynolds, Winston A. "The Burning Ships of Hernán Cortés." *Hispania*, vol. 42, no. 3, 1959, pp. 317–324. *JSTOR*, www.jstor.org/stable/335707. Accessed 31 July 2021.

5. Quotes. https://www.quotes.net/movies/tin_cup_11675. Retrieved 7-31-21.

6. "Listen to your Heart" by Roxette. Songfacts. https://www.songfacts.com/facts/roxette/listen-to-your-heart. Retrieved 7-31-21.

7. Lindström, Sven (2002). *The Ballad Hits* (CD liner notes). Roxette. Capitol Records.

8. *The Great Gatsby*. F. Scott Fitzgerald. Scribner. 2020. New York, NY. Page 48.

9. "Kevin Love: 'For me a form of therapy or feeling better is practicing acts of kindness.'" Adam Renuart. April 25th, 2020. CNN. https://www.cnn.com/2020/04/25/sport/nba-kevin-love-coronavirus-mental-health-spt-intl/index.html. Retrieved 7-31-21.

10. "Washington takes command of Continental Army in 1775." U.S. Army Center of Military History. April 15, 2016. US Army. https://www.army.mil/article/40819/washington_takes_command_of_continental_army_in_1775. Retrieved 7-31-21.

Chapter 3

1. Quotes. https://www.quotes.net/movies/tin_cup_11675. Retrieved 7-31-21.
2. *The Formative Years at Atlanta's Westminster Schools.* William Pressly. McGuire Publishing Company. 1991. Page 15.
3. *Winners Dream: A Journey from Corner Store to Corner Office.* Bill McDermott. Page 6. Simon & Schuster. 2014.
4. *A First-Rate Madness: Uncovering the Links Between Leadership and Mental Illness.* Nassir Ghaemi. Penguin. New York. 2011. Page 247-48.
5. *The 7 Habits of Highly Effective People: Powerful Lessons in Personal Change.* Stephen Covey. Simon & Schuster. New York. 2013.
6. Bill McDermott and students at SAP Next Gen Hudson Yard. April 26th, 2017. https://www.youtube.com/watch?v=KDP34LFOO_k Retrieved 7-31-21.
7. "Quotes About Listening." https://www.leadershipnow.com/listeningquotes.html. LeadershipNow. Retrieved 7-31-21.
8. *Leadership.* James McGregor Burns. Harper Perennial Classics. New York. 2010.
9. Bill McDermott and students at SAP Next Gen Hudson Yard. April 26th, 2017. https://www.youtube.com/watch?v=KDP34LFOO_k Retrieved 7-31-21.
10. Isaiah 6:1-8. *Holy Bible.* Page 1068.
11. "10 Quotes to Inspire Active Listening."

https://www.roberthalf.com/blog/salaries-and-skills/10-quotes-to-inspire-active-listening. Robert Half Talent Solutions. Retrieved 7-31-21.

12. *Lincoln on Leadership: Executive Strategies for Tough Times.* Donald Phillips. 1992. Warner Books. New York. Page 35-36.

Chapter 4

1. Genesis 22:1-19. *Holy Bible.* Page 31.
2. Proverbs 3: 5-6. *Holy Bible.* Page 987.
3. "7 Leadership Lessons From the CEO of a Multibillion-Dollar Company
   SAP CEO Bill McDermott is doing it his way--and it's working. Here are seven lessons you can learn from him." April 3rd, 2017. https://www.inc.com/john-eades/7-leadership-lessons-from-the-ceo-of-a-multi-billion-dollar-company.html. Retrieved 7-31-21.
4. "SAP's CEO on Why Trust Is the Ultimate Career Weapon." Bill McDermott. November 13th, 2014. Bloomberg. https://www.bloomberg.com/news/articles/2014-11-13/saps-ceo-to-succeed-at-business-redefine-success. Retrieved 7-31-21.
5. "Authenticity-Bing Definition" https://www.bing.com/search?q=authenticity+definition&qs=LS&pq=authenticity+&sc=8-13&cvid=475466F0AC5B46A9BADA32DB2787BC83&FORM=QBRE&sp=1 Retrieved 7-31-21.
6. Maclean. Page 16.

7. *Mediations.* Marcus Aurelius. Barnes and Noble. New York, NY. 2003. Page 52.
8. Proverbs 27:17. *Holy Bible.* Page 987.
9. *Maxims of George Washington.* Mount Vernon Ladies' Association. 1989. Mt. Vernon, VA.
10. Proverbs 1:5. *Holy Bible.* Page 984.
11. "You Oughta Remember." Jason Radford. March 31, 2011. http://popstache.com/features/old-stache/alanis-morissette-jagged-little-pill-review/ Retrieved 7-31-21.

Chapter 5

1. Quotes. https://www.quotes.net/movies/tin_cup_11675. Retrieved 7-31-21.
2. "On an Epic Winning Streak." Osayi Endolyn. July 30th, 2015. Georgia Tech News Center. https://www.news.gatech.edu/2015/07/30/epic-winning-streak Retrieved 7-31-21.
3. Joshua 1:9. *Holy Bible.* Page 332.
4. Quotes. https://www.quotes.net/movies/tin_cup_11675. Retrieved 7-31-21.
5. Joshua 1:9. *Holy Bible.* Page 1567.
6. Maclean. Page 103.
7. "First Ladies Influence and Image: Rosalynn Carter."http://firstladies.c-span.org/FirstLady/41/Rosalynn-Carter.aspx. Retrieved 7-30-21.

Chapter 6

1. *To Obama: With love, joy, anger and hope.* Jeanne Marie Laskas. Random House. New York, NY. 2018. Page 48-52.
2. "Wisdom Isn't What You Think It Is: It's more about listening than talking." David Brooks. April 15th, 2021.*The New York Times.* https://www.nytimes.com/2021/04/15/opinion/wisdom-attention-listening.html. Retrieved 8-1-21.
3. "Obama angers midwest voters with guns and religion remark." Ed Pilkington. April 14th, 2008. *The Guardian.* https://www.theguardian.com/world/2008/apr/14/barackobama.uselections2008. Retrieved 8-1-21.
4. "Obama hits back at Clinton amid 'bitter' flap." The Associated Press. April 12th, 2008. *NBC News.* https://www.nbcnews.com/id/wbna24082427. Retrieved 8-1-21.
5. "Obama's 2006 Speech on Faith and Politics." June 28th, 2006. *The New York Times.* https://www.nytimes.com/2006/06/28/us/politics/2006obamaspeech.html. Retrieved 8-1-21.
6. *To Kill A Mockingbird.* Harper Lee. Hachette Book Group. New York, NY. 2010. Page 39.
7. *To Kill a Mockingbird.* 1962. Universal Pictures.
8. Maren Morris – The Bones (Story Behind the Song.) MarenMorrisVEVO. August 17th, 2019. https://www.youtube.com/watch?v=fc8ANwDjX3s. Retrieved 8-1-21.

9. "The Bones." Maren Morris Lyrics. https://www.azlyrics.com/lyrics/maren-morris/thebones.html. Retrieved 8-1-21.
10. Asia Youth International Model United Nations. https://modelunitednation.org/about. Retrieved 8-1-21.
11. "Nancy Reagan: First Lady Nancy Reagan described her deep love of Ronald Reagan and admonished young women who were fearful of commitment." *The Saturday Evening Post*: Special Collector's Edition. June 2020. Page 40.
12. *Jane Eyre*. Charlotte Brontë. Barnes & Noble Classics. New York. 2003. Page 130.
13. "Bill McDermott takes reins as ServiceNow CEO sooner than expected with new CFO." Ron Miller. November 18th, 2019. *Tech Crunch*. https://techcrunch.com/2019/11/18/bill-mcdermott-takes-reins-as-servicenow-ceo-sooner-than-expected-with-new-cfo/. Retrieved 8-1-21.
14. Song of Songs 2:3. *Holy Bible*. Page 1051.
15. Romans 7:4-5. *Holy Bible*. 1755.

Chapter 7

1. "Eudora Welty – Quotes – Quotable Quote" https://www.goodreads.com/quotes/16088-indeed-learning-to-write-may-be-part-of-learning-to. Retrieved 8-1-21.
2. "Sarah Bush Lincoln (William H. Herndon Interview)". September 8th, 1865. https://digital.lib.niu.edu/islandora/object/niu-lincoln%3A34912. Retrieved 8-1-21.

3. "History Faceoff: Who Was the Greatest President—Washington or Lincoln? As Presidents' Day approaches, two preeminent historians join the enduring debate about whether George Washington or Abraham Lincoln was America's greatest president." Christopher Klein. February 15th, 2017. *History.com.* https://www.history.com/news/history-faceoff-who-was-the-greatest-president-washington-or-lincoln. Retrieved 8-1-21.
4. Brooks. Page 211.
5. Phillips. Page 100.

Chapter 8

1. Thomas Jefferson, The Papers of Thomas Jefferson, Volume 16: November 1789 to July 1790.
2. "Happy Gilmore." Quotes. https://www.quotes.net/movies/happy_gilmore_4959 Retrieved 8-1-21.
3. Genesis 3:1-24. *Holy Bible.* Page 5-6.

Chapter 9

1. *Things Fall Apart.* Chinua Achebe. Penguin. New York, NY. 2017. Page 3.
2. Achebe. Page 4.
3. Job 1:21. *Holy Bible.* Page 789-90.
4. Hebrews 12: 11. *Holy Bible.* Page 1877.
5. Langford, Joe; Clance, Pauline Rose (Fall 1993). "The impostor phenomenon: recent research findings regarding dynamics,

personality and family patterns and their implications for treatment" Psychotherapy: Theory, Research, Practice, Training. 30 (3): 495–501.

6. Jeremiah 1:5. *Holy Bible*. Page 1169.

7. "Mattis breaks silence: 'I had no choice but to leave'; George Washington is my model." Laura Widener. August 29th, 2019. https://americanmilitarynews.com/2019/08/mattis-breaks-silence-i-had-no-choice-but-to-leave-george-washington-is-my-model/. *American Military News*. Retrieved 8-1-21.

8. "Leaders: Do You Know How to Listen." Jarret Jackson. *Forbes*. July 29th, 2020. https://www.forbes.com/sites/jarretjackson/2020/07/29/leaders-do-you-know-how-to-listen/?sh=4d230f1734ab. Retrieved 8-1-21.

9. *The Second Mountain: The Quest for a Moral Life*. David Brooks. Random House New York. 2019. Page xxii.

10. "To James Madison from Thomas Jefferson, 16 September 1821," Founders Online, National Archives, https://founders.archives.gov/documents/Madison/04-02-02-0322. [Original source: The Papers of James Madison, Retirement Series, vol. 2, 1 February 1820–26 February 1823, ed. David B. Mattern, J. C. A. Stagg, Mary Parke Johnson, and Anne Mandeville Colony. Charlottesville: University of Virginia Press, 2013, pp. 382–383.]

11. Source – Bing Dictionary. https://www.bing.com/search?q=source&cvid=51e0c90b22224dc1a114a2d5b433d70c&aqs=edge..69i57j0l4j69i60l2.6359j0j1&pglt=43&FORM=ANNTA1&PC=HCTS. Retrieved 8-1-21.

Chapter 10

1. "Happy Gilmore." Quotes. https://www.quotes.net/movies/happy_gilmore_4959 Retrieved 8-1-21.
2. Proverbs 1:32-33. *Holy Bible.* Page 986.
3. Luke 14:25-33. *Holy Bible.* Page 1623.
4. "Why am I here?" Bibletract.org. http://www.bibletract.org/studies/purpose_1.pdf. Retrieved 8-1-21.
5. "Sacrifice." https://www.lexico.com/definition/sacrifice. Retrieved 8-1-21.
6. Achebe. Page 26.
7. Achebe. Page 28.
8. Achebe. Page 63-5.
9. Romans 6:1-23. *Holy Bible.* Page 1754-5.
10. Maclean. Page 1.
11. "Life of Faith." Timothy J. Keller. January 26th, 2021. https://gospelinlife.com/downloads/life-of-faith-5825/. Retrieved 8-1-21.

Chapter 11

1. "Einstein On Creative Thinking: Music and the Intuitive Art of Scientific Imagination: Einstein explored time and space… in his musical hobbies." Michele and Robert Root-Bernstein. *Psychology Today.* https://www.psychologytoday.com/us/blog/imagine/201003/einst

ein-creative-thinking-music-and-the-intuitive-art-scientific-imagination. March 31ˢᵗ, 2010. Retrieved 8-1-21.

2. John 8:32. *Holy Bible.* Page 1663.

3. "The Sound of Music - Sixteen Going On Seventeen Lyrics." Song Lyrics. http://www.songlyrics.com/thesound-of-music/sixteen-going-on-seventeen-lyrics/. Retrieved 8-1-21.

4. "Believers in the Bible." https://www.ucg.org/bible-study-tools/bible-study-course/bible-study-course-lesson-1/believers-in-the-bible. February 16ᵗʰ, 2011.

5. "Fact-checking Romney's '47 percent' comment." Lucy Madison. *CBS News.* September 25ᵗʰ, 2012. https://www.cbsnews.com/news/fact-checking-romneys-47-percent-comment/. Retrieved 8-1-21.

6. "Mitt Romney: '95% Of Life Is Set Up For You If You're Born In This Country.'" Ryan Grim and Arthur Delaney. *HuffPost.* September 20ᵗʰ, 2012. https://www.huffpost.com/entry/mitt-romney-95-percent-video_n_1900608. Retrieved 8-1-21.

7. "Why Mitt Romney's '47 percent' comment was so bad." Chris Cilliza. *The Washington Post.* March 4ᵗʰ, 2013. https://www.washingtonpost.com/news/the-fix/wp/2013/03/04/why-mitt-romneys-47-percent-comment-was-so-bad/. Retrieved 8-1-21.

8. 1ˢᵗ Corinthians 9:20. *Holy Bible.* Page 1781.

9. "Gone, Gone. Gone." Phillip Phillips. Genuis. https://genius.com/Phillip-phillips-gone-gone-gone-lyrics. Retrieved 8-1-21.

10. "15 Quotes to Inspire You to Become a Better Listener: Listening skills are vital to your success in business -- and in life. For a fresh perspective, consider these insights from the

world's great thinkers." Dave Kerpen. *Inc.* January 9th, 2014. https://www.inc.com/dave-kerpen/15-quotes-to-inspire-you-to-become-a-better-listener.html. Retrieved 8-1-21.

11. Grady Smith (December 19, 2012). "Phillip Phillips announces next single https://ew.com/article/2012/12/19/phillip-phillips-announces-next-single-gone-gone-gone-hear-it-here/'Gone Gone Gone': Hear it here!". EW.com. Retrieved 8-1-21.

12. "Gone, Gone. Gone." Phillip Phillips. Genuis. https://genius.com/Phillip-phillips-gone-gone-gone-lyrics. Retrieved 8-1-21.

13. "Gone, Gone, Gone – Phillip Phillips." http://www.musicinsideu.com/2013/05/gone-gone-gone-phillip-phillips.html. Retrieved 8-1-21.

14. Diplo Says 'Lean On' Was Initially Meant for Nicki Minaj or Rihanna

15. "He calls the stars passing on it a 'blessing in disguise.'" Brennan Carley. *Spin.* August 19th, 2015. https://www.spin.com/2015/08/diplo-mo-major-lazer-lean-on-rihanna-nicki-minaj-dj-snake/. Retrieved 8-1-21.

16. "Lean On: Major Lazer." https://genius.com/Major-lazer-lean-on-lyrics#:~:text=%E2%80%9CLean%20On%E2%80%9D%20is%20the%20lead%20single%20from%20and,about%20the%20exhilaration%20and%20disappointment%20of%20young%20love.. Retrieved 8-1-21.

17. Jeremiah 29:12 *Holy Bible.* 1221.

18. Whitburn, Joel (2004). Top R&B/Hip-Hop Singles: 1942-2004. Record Research. p. 633.
19. "The RS 500 Greatest Songs of All Time." *Rolling Stone*. December 9th, 2004. https://web.archive.org/web/20080625061023/http://www.rollingstone.com/news/coverstory/500songs/page/3. Retrieved 8-1-21.
20. "Bill Withers." *Songfacts*. https://www.songfacts.com/blog/interviews/bill-withers. Retrieved 8-1-21.
21. Acts 4:32-35. *Holy Bible*. Page 1697.

Chapter 12

1. *Uncle Tom's Cabin: Or, Life Among the Lowly*. Harriet Beecher Stowe. Random House. 2000. Page 402.
2. "Cardigan – Taylor Swift." https://genius.com/Taylor-swift-cardigan-lyrics. Retrieved 8-1-21.
3. "Mercy – Dave Matthews Lyrics." https://www.azlyrics.com/lyrics/davematthews/mercy.html. Retrieved 8-1-21.
4. Stowe. Page 423-25.
5. Stowe. Page 350.
6. Stowe. Page 334.
7. *Letter From Birmingham Jail*. Martin Luther King Jr. Penguin UK. 2018.
8. Matthew 20:16. *Holy Bible*. 1530.
9. Stowe. Page 391.
10. Stowe. Page 410-11.

Chapter 13

1. "Happy Gilmore." Quotes. https://www.quotes.net/movies/happy_gilmore_4959 Retrieved 8-1-21.
2. Michael Burlingame, Abraham Lincoln: A Life (2 volumes, originally published by Johns Hopkins University Press, 2008) Unedited Manuscript By Chapters, Lincoln Studies Center, Volume 1, Chapter 6 (PDF), pp. 547-548.
3. Morrison, Jago. "Tradition and Modernity in Chinua Achebe's African Trilogy." Research in African Literatures, vol. 49, no. 4, 2018, pp. 14–26. JSTOR, www.jstor.org/stable/10.2979/reseafrilite.49.4.03. Accessed 1 Aug. 2021.
4. "Black kids go missing at a higher rate than white kids. Here's why we don't hear about them." Harmeet Kaur. CNN. November 3rd, 2019. https://www.cnn.com/2019/11/03/us/missing-children-of-color-trnd/index.html. Retrieved 8-1-21.
5. Achebe. 176.
6. Achebe. 207-9.

From the Pages of *Forget Self-Help: Re-Examining the Golden Rule*

Nonetheless, when someone bears our burdens with us, often a huge weight lifts from our shoulders. Does this mean that the other person can solve the problem that the other one is going through? *No.* However, just knowing that someone cares enough to forget his *own* problems and focus on *yours* is reassuring. **—CHAPTER 1**

When people speak of having an advantage over someone, they often feel as if they have to tread on sharp glass. There is no need to do this because none of us created our own advantages. They were given to us by God. However, we do need to tread lightly on how we use our own advantages to help others. **—CHAPTER 2**

Usually, when we ourselves are in a position of power, we like to look to see how we can use it to control others instead of realizing that we need to control ourselves that much more because of the position we are now in. **—CHAPTER 2**

A man's heart is only strong when it is safe, and it is only safe when it is secured in something strong. **—CHAPTER 2**

Since none of us will see God on Earth, we face an uphill battle to show others that God truly exists.**—CHAPTER 3**

One reason that we never get to know other people is because it requires us to become vulnerable to other people. To become vulnerable not only requires work but also requires courage. Many people are unwilling to admit their blind spots or flaws. However, when this happens, a whole new world is opened up because it enables both parties to be real with each other.—**CHAPTER 4**

Without loving oneself first, it is impossible to love others. — **CHAPTER 4**

Everyone can agree though that anything worthwhile, anything worth striving for, has some element of rarity to it.—**CHAPTER 5**

When judging another person, I never look for the big moments that test their character. I look for the small ones. Big moments carry a heroic aspect to them so there is a certain selfish incentive to make sure they are carried out to fruition. Small moments, however, never get any credit. This accentuates their value. —**CHAPTER 6**

We need to be extreme. We need to be bold. We need to go all out. But we need to do this all for others, not ourselves. —**CHAPTER 6**

The best way to tell if someone is with you is to see whether a person will help you even if he knows he will get nothing in return from you. Anyone can help when there is something to gain in return; to help when there is nothing to be gained shows true love. —**CHAPTER 7**

Showing mercy toward others is not an easy task. It requires patience, humility, and an inverse style of thinking that goes against our natural selfish desires. It also requires giving up a sense of control, a sense of control we often feel like we earned in the first place. —**CHAPTER 7**

Holding someone accountable for their actions can be one of the most delicate and awkward dealings that a human being has to do for another. But in strong relationships, this happens frequently. —
CHAPTER 8

So many times, we lash out against others when they give us advice or critique our actions. We need to realize they are doing so because they believe in us and think we are capable of greatness. **—CHAPTER 8**

When we do for others, we provide more happiness for ourselves more effectively than when we try to focus only on ourselves. The reason for this is simple: putting ourselves in another's shoes makes us forget all about our own problems. **—CHAPTER 8**

What happens when we focus less on ourselves and instead devote that energy toward others? We benefit others and also benefit ourselves. When we reach out to someone who is in need, we fulfill the words of Christ. By following the Golden Rule in our attitude, behavior, and conduct, we make the world a better place and make our own lives better too. **—CONCLUSION**

You only love someone when you are willing to sacrifice for them; without sacrifice, there is no love. **—CONCLUSION**

From the Pages of *The Criminal: The Power of An Apology*

Failing at an early age produces character, determination, and humility, all of which can never be learned without it. If you do fail, however, it means you had the courage to take a risk, which is in itself, quite admirable **– CHAPTER 1**

Failing should be thought of like a photograph. You see it, but only for the instant in which the image was captured. Photography can be misleading, just like failing. **– CHAPTER 1**

Failing is not failure; how you react to your failure is the indication of whether you have truly failed or not. **– CHAPTER 1**

Courage often is a result of failure in the same way that success is a result of courage; therefore, to achieve success in life, you have to overcome failure with courage. **– CHAPTER 1**

The only way to be found is to admit we are lost. **– CHAPTER 2**

We all hope; it is what we hope for that demonstrates where our true heart is. All the criminal hoped for is to be found again; in his repentance and in his character, that happened. **– CHAPTER 2**

With Christianity, the less you are in control, the more you are in control. **– CHAPTER 2**

The nice thing about knowing that Jesus died for our sins is that once we know that simple truth, our lives are transformed.

Sin in no longer chasing us; we know longer have to dodge and weave to hide: we are free, but only if we admit our sin. –
CHAPTER 2

In making yourself vulnerable to the ones you love, a foundation as solid as a rock is formed. – **CHAPTER 2**

Admitting your blind spot is a challenging thing to, but it produces a realness is relationships, because it shows the person you know that you are only human. That humbleness opens the door for them to be humble back to you, opening the way for a deeper form of communication than you thought was possible. –
CHAPTER 2

I often find myself trying to be perfect, and when I'm not, I find myself trying to cover up my sin when I should be doing the opposite because Christ died for me. – **CHAPTER 2**

The last thing I like to do is admit that I am wrong, but when I do, I know God is smiling; after all, it means my complete trust is in him. – **CHAPTER 2**

To God however, beauty means admitting we are broken and lost, needing to pick up God's rhythms to regain it. Whatever we do is not enough because we have all fallen short, so very short of his Glory. Only in the cross, can we regain that beauty. –
CHAPTER 2

The opposite of sarcasm is vulnerability. You can tell when a man is strong when he is more attuned to the latter rather than the former. – **CHAPTER 3**

Without integrity, a person is empty. The emptiness comes from that person's lack of respect for reality; in life, reality accounts for everything that is worthwhile. – **CHAPTER 4**

To make a difference, we have to make a change. The reason for this is rather simple: we are all fallen—in need of his saving grace– **CHAPTER 4**

It is only when we hide our sin that we get into trouble. Admitting your trouble is the surest way to get out of trouble in Christianity. – **CHAPTER 4**

Being honest doesn't require you to be good-looking, smart, or clever, it only requires showing your authentic self to the world. Chances are, if you are honest, people will appreciate you more, listen to you more, and value you more. The reason for this is simple: you will now be set apart in a rare class. – **CHAPTER 4**

To take it learning even further, one has to learn from anybody and everybody, even the flawed. In doing so, your life will be changed, and once your life is changed, you will change others. – **CHAPTER 5**

Only when we admit that we are less, and He is more, will we be found. The reason for this simple: admitting that we are less doesn't make us *less*, it makes us *more*. – **CHAPTER 5**

With power, often comes pride. That pride is not from above, but down below. The only thing we need to be prideful of is what Jesus did for us on the cross. It was the opposite of prideful. Because of this, it was definition of powerful. **– CHAPTER 5**

Jesus never seeks earthly might. To be a king is to be rich, powerful, carry a good name, and have lots of servants. I guess Jesus never got the memo. For him, power was in being *with* us, not *over* us. **– CHAPTER 5**

Most people are too proud to learn, but the most impactful of people always take the position that in order to impact people, you can never learn enough. **– CHAPTER 5**

We're blessed in that when Jesus said, "It is finished", what it meant for us is that it was only getting started. Through his death on the cross, we could start to love again, start to matter again, but most of all, we could start to heal again. In healing again, we can start to live again. And we are doubly blessed in that most leaders close their doors. Most famous people try to avoid the paparazzi and fans. Not Jesus though. He told us he would be with us until the end of the age. **– CHAPTER 5**

We are all fake, all lost, void of anything worthwhile without the blood of Jesus. We all need blood in order to survive. Why live only to survive, why not live to thrive? We can, but only with the blood of Jesus. Only his blood is pure, that is for certain. **– CHAPTER 6**

When we repent, we are secure. It's a security that is much more comforting than a 401K or a seat-belt in a car. It's a security that transcends all understanding, and once you have it, all you want to do is pass it on. After all, to give that security is to give life. And it's not just life on this earth, it's life everlasting. – **CHAPTER 6**

I need Jesus' blood just as I need oxygen, food, water, and shelter. Without it, I can never survive, never thrive. Without it I am a nobody, I can achieve nothing. With it, I am not only powerful, I am free. – **CHAPTER 6**

We're often taught to present our best self to the world even though deep down we know this is not for the best. – **CHAPTER 6**

You can tell how much someone believes in the cross by how open they are about their own sin. – **CHAPTER 6**

Thankfulness shouldn't be situation-based because difficult times have a way of shaping us in a stronger, more effective way than a seemingly encouraging time. It's more challenging to grow when things are going well. When you're at the very bottom, upward is the only direction you can go. – **CHAPTER 6**

To be thankful isn't to walk around with a smile on your face all the time. Jesus didn't have a smile on his face when he was crucified. After all, didn't he cry out, "why have you forsaken me?" He did have the wherewithal to trust God during that time, however. When you trust in God during the toughest of times, He credits that as thankfulness. – **CHAPTER 8**

For me, gratitude can frame meaningless drudgery into meaningful opportunities."

Disciple is the root word of discipline. So why is discipline seen as an *extremely* negative word and disciple as an extremely *positive* word? – **CHAPTER 9**

It might seem like a paradox, but you want to try to be a person that no one wants to be around because when he leaves your presence they are immediately disappointed by the decreased level of character and encouragement they are now forced to be around in terms of dealing with other people. – **CHAPTER 9**

I challenge the people I respect, but to those who have neither the capacity nor ability to change, I am silent. – **CHAPTER 9**

The criminal serves as a guide to us all. He's humble, yet unafraid, clever, without the usual pretentiousness; but most of all, he is loyal, and in his loyalty, he became the first convert to Christianity; in doing so, he joined Jesus in paradise forever. – **CONCLUSION**

From the Pages of *He Spoke with Authority: Get, then Give the Advantage of Confidence*

It made me realize two things: to be happy for another person's success doesn't make you *less* of a person, it makes you *more* of a person. It also made me realize that the common perception that a true friend is one who is with you during the worst of times is wrong. A friend who is with you during the best of your times is truly there for you for he is not jealous, but happy for you, showing true love. - **CHAPTER 1**

All of us should have the utmost confidence in ourselves for one primary reason: what Jesus did for us on the cross. Once we realize that, indeed, we are made perfect by His actions, we can shake off all the insecurities that hold us back and start to live for Him. It's tough for us to comprehend this because we live in such a merit-based society; luckily for, our merit was earned by Jesus' blood on the cross. Nothing else can make us more whole or secure. – **CHAPTER 1**

People are going to doubt you if you possess the courage to do anything great. Let them do so: chances are they are jealous that you have the guts and talent to try. – **CHAPTER 1**

It's okay to think that you are capable of greatness. That's not a sin in God's eyes. Just make sure you are using your talents and so forth for God's glory, not just your own. The scariest scenario for the Devil is to have a confident God-fearing human carrying out the Lord's work. The Devil is not at all scared of insecure Christ followers; in fact, that's who he takes advantage of the most. **– CHAPTER 2**

Don't let others lead you down your own path; let God do that; God knew you first. **– CHAPTER 2**

We can bring heaven here on earth, but only when we display confidence in ourselves. Sitting on the sidelines is futile. **– CHAPTER 2**

Do yourself a favor: let the force of confidence get you moving. When you do, you will move others and, in the process, be moved yourself. **– CHAPTER 2**

For parents to stifle their child's optimism is to not only stifle their own dreams, but the dreams of others. The reason for this is simple: once one achieves their own dreams, they often help others to achieve their own dreams; at least the great ones do. **– CHAPTER 2**

Protectors are able to protect us because the security they have in themselves; they refuse to be insecure because they know they have to be secure for others. **- CHAPTER 2**

The Bible tells us that to much has been given, much is expected; go into your day knowing that you have been entrusted with much and it is all for His glory, not just for your own pleasure. With this new way of thinking, you'll find that your pleasure becomes His glory. Ultimately, you know your faith is strong when you say "thank you" to God, and God says, "no, *thank you.*" This means that your purpose in life and His will are one in the same. – **CHAPTER 2**

There is nothing more noble than sticking up for someone else when they have been wronged. There is one characteristic that a human being must have to do this: confidence. Sticking up for yourself is easy, but to stick up for another human being shows a blend of both unselfishness and confidence which the mother and father of what Christianity is all about. – **CHAPTER 3**

You can't always be safe and confident at the same time. And chances are if you are too confident, you are doing something that is too safe. - **CHAPTER 3**

When you're the only one that can stick up for yourself, do so with courage and you may just find the respect of the people who have tried to trample you down. At the very least, they may find some empathy for the situation. – **CHAPTER 3**

Security in oneself leads to security in the other person. It shows that you are humble, not so much putting the weight of the world in yourself, but ultimately others. If you're secure with yourself, you'll find yourself reaching out to make sure other people are secure with themselves. In doing so, you'll become that much more secure with yourself. - **CHAPTER 3**

When you find yourself sticking up for people more and more, you know that you are growing more and more confident; the insecure, however, only stick up for themselves. – **CHAPTER 3**

Other's affliction should affect all of us, and when it does, you know you're confident in your own skin. - **CHAPTER 3**

While it is noble to turn the other cheek, when another person is hurting you so much to the point where you have trouble living, it is not only okay to stick up for yourself, but God wants you to do so; he wants you to be strong so you can do His work. – **CHAPTER 3**

Getting out of abusive relationships is hard, but necessary. When you're in an abusive relationship, it is impossible to carry out God's will the best you can because in the back of your mind you're filled with all the trauma of the abusive relationship. – **CHAPTER 3**

Whatever seems unlikely, improbable, even if something has never happened before, it can happen through God. Is it okay to be nervous knowing that you are chosen by God to do his work? Yes, but just know that by putting your confidence in Him, you will in turn be more confident, being able to accomplish anything for Him. – **CHAPTER 4**

Once we have confidence in Him, he gives us all the confidence we need to do His work. God wants you to be confident; He knows that without it, the mission he has set before us will never be accomplished. – **CHAPTER 4**

When we look out for others, our confidence shows in plain light and cannot be hidden. God gave us confidence so we could save others just as He saved us on the cross. Once this shift of perspective in your thinking happens, you will be bolder, thus changing more lives. – **CHAPTER 4**

Confidence is like centrifugal force; it is never ceasing, it always extends to the receiver and back to the giver. It doesn't just unlock doors, it tears them down off its hinges so it will be easier for the next person walk through; or, better yet, run through. – **CHAPTER 4**

Confident people often sacrifice themselves so that the rest of us cannot only live but live well; these people aren't so bad after all, for they lived as Jesus lived.; they sacrifice just as Jesus sacrificed.- **CHAPTER 4**

When you're vulnerable with someone, there is a connection that cannot be broken. In laying down all your cards, you'll discover that you have the winning hand. The reason you win is by allowing the other person to see you clearly for the first time— allowing them to assist you when you need assistance, cry with you when you feel you need comfort, and help you stand when you feel as if you cannot bear your own weight. – **CHAPTER 5**

To be vulnerable is to be real, and in that vulnerability, you are strong. - **CHAPTER 5**

Intimacy is like that tough conversation that you don't want to have: you dread it, during it you're scared and frightened, but afterwards you're telling yourself: I can't wait to come back for more. The next time though, you dread it less, thus enabling you to be even more intimate; once again; after you've experienced it, you come back for more. - **CHAPTER 5**

What does having a mentor say about somebody? Well, ultimately, it shows that they are both confident and humble—two words that rarely go together. It shows that you are humble enough to feel that you *need* to improve and confident enough that you *can* improve. - **CHAPTER 6**

Confidence leads to empathy because of the security you have in yourself. With that security, you can give it to others who need it. – **CHAPTER 6**

To be a strong Christian, you must emit a different type of electricity to others. It's a type of electricity that only comes from confidence. You'll often find that once you emit that electricity toward others, you will get just as much back. – **CHAPTER 7**

Real love is not silent; it speaks to us in a way we are not used to hearing; therefore, there is no way to mute it like we turn like we mute TV commercials. Real love is strong, bold, courageous, and confident; it teaches us to dare in its daringness. – **CHAP-TER 8**

From the Pages of *Mrs. Dubose's Last Wish*

We all suffer from time to time in our lives, some more than others. It's how we react to that suffering that separates the winners from the losers. – **CHAPTER 1**

The strongest predictor of success is the amount of suffering one is willing to embrace. – **CHAPTER 1**

To want to fight after enduring so much pain, you have to not only outlast until the final bell rings, but you also have to overcome trials and tribulations that seem like they will go on forever. – **CHAPTER 1**

When we are on the ground and can't stand up, we tend to think God has forgotten about us. This couldn't be further from the truth because God uses painful experiences not only to build us up, but also others around us. – **CHAPTER 1**

When our complete trust is in God, we have no choice but to thank God for whatever happens, knowing firmly that *He*, and not *we*, has the best handle on our lives. – **CHAPTER 1**

Whatever you are going through at the present time, just know that—believe it or not—God knows what you are going through, and, better yet, he knows what you have to do to get through to the finish line. – **CHAPTER 2**

Whatever you are going through, fear should not have a place in your heart because The Lord is by your side just as a best friend is with you through your worst times, and He is your number one cheerleader during your best times, or, in this digital age, the first one to post your success on social media. He is not afraid to sacrifice for you, even if it means going through a painful, gruesome death on a wooden cross for you. He's already gone through that pain, so that you can have pain no more. – **CHAPTER 2**

When someone tells you that they want you to see something, they're telling you that because they feel as if you have not noticed something that they think would be beneficial for you to see; more than likely, something to make you grow. – **CHAPTER 2**

When I think of someone who is worthy of respect, I immediately think of someone who is hard on themselves. To earn the respect of all, one must be hard on himself. The moment he lets go of this plight, is the moment he begins to lose the respect of many, if not all. – **CHAPTER 3**

I've realized that the most influential don't mind suffering themselves, but if they're even put in a position where they can alleviate another's suffering, they'll do so every single time, often in a hurry. – **CHAPTER 3**

When we love unconditionally—without getting anything back in return—we end up getting just as much back, if not more. The quicker others pain becomes yours is the barometer of how sensitive you are, and, contrary to popular belief, being sensitive is not a sign of weakness, but strength. – **CHAPTER 3**

Suffering isn't easy and *choosing* to suffer is even harder. But in life, we must choose to suffer if we ever want anything accomplished. – **CHAPTER 4**

It is alright for us to pray to God to alleviate our suffering, but only if it furthers his kingdom or will. If you can do that, you know you are on the path to a close relationship with The Lord. – **CHAPTER 4**

If what you're about to attempt doesn't scare you, what you're attempting to do is not of insignificance. Signs on the highway show significant landmarks such as places to eat, stay, and be entertained. Let what you're striving after show the signs of significance as well. – **CHAPTER 4**

Only when you begin to choose to suffer from time to time do you know your faith is catching on. If you find yourself seeking pleasure all the time instead of pain, check yourself because not only do sacrifice and suffering start with the same letter, they both bring a smile to God. – **CHAPTER 6**

When you're suffering, you naturally think that first and foremost you must dig yourself out of a hole, when in actuality, digging other people out of a hole can prove to be much more effective for alleviating that suffering – **CHAPTER 6**

In many ways we can't choose the fate that God has given us. Some of us are born tall, some of us are born short, some of us white, some of us black. What we can do, however, is react to what God has given us because he has given us free-will. We are not robots programmed by God; we have choices. Whatever problems you are going through, know that in the end, you have a choice as to how you will react to it. – **CHAPTER 6**

Our first inclination is look out for ourselves when we are suffering, and, when we do so, it often causes us to forget to look out for the needs of others. Christ, on the other hand, got hurt on the cross so he could *help* people. He didn't have to do so, but he wanted to make us whole again. – **CHAPTER 6**

Sometimes, the reason God wants us to suffer is to get that big part of us that is off the track back on the rails. He does this because this is the only way we will be able to see what we are doing wrong. Are you wise enough to realize this? I hope so. – **CHAPTER 6**

Life is very reactionary; those who react with the most bravery during the most harrowing times are the ones who are remembered. In debates, politicians, are taught by their debate coaches not to react in a negative way even if their competitors are trying to get under their skin. – **CHAPTER 6**

From the Pages of *When I See It: Belief in the Uncertainty*

Laughter dampens our woes in a way that it not only stops the pain, but gives a chance to learn from it, thus enabling us to be stronger the next time. – **CHAPTER 2**

Shift your reason for happiness based on *other's* happiness instead of your *own*, and you will be more fulfilled; I guarantee it. – **CHAPTER 2**

"When you're given something, you've got to pass it... pass it on, pass it around, or pass it backwards. Not to do so is not only unappreciative, but also an insult to God." – **CHAPTER 2**

It's not just that when one door closes, another opens, often times you'll that when your door opens, you'll get to have the opportunity to open that same door for others— creating an environment that never could have happened if that originally door hadn't been closed. Having a door closed only means God is going to present you with an opportunity to open more doors for others—and Him—in the future. **– CHAPTER 2**

We are often fearful of what we don't know because fear is often born out of ignorance; the worst part of this is that it can lead to quick judgment—most the time that judgment being wrong. **– CHAPTER 3**

How is it that fail to see people for who they really are more often than not? Is it pride, is it pain? Or insecurity? As human beings, we are all so different, but nonetheless so similar in the fact that we often succumb to the mistake of rushing judgment on one another, and even if we don't rush that judgment, we often make the mistake of judging one another on inconsequential aspects of our life instead of things that matter. **– CHAPTER 3**

The cover—or the outside—distracts us from seeing what's on the inside more often than not even though it contains no content—or, nothing to learn from. When people refer to what percentage of a book they've read, they often describe their progress in the number of pages read. They're telling you how much content they have gotten through; only then can they truly judge a book. Judge people in the same way. Count the pages you've read before you start drawing conclusions. **– CHAPTER 3**

Layers in a cake can be challenging to read because if you look from the top down, you can't see that there are even layers in the first place; it just seems like there is one consistency in whatever it is you're looking at. But it you see the cake at eye level, you'll soon see a cake for what it's really worth—the whole picture. To see the whole picture, you must be at eye-level, meaning that you're willing to look at the cake in the same way it glances back at you. In the same way, humans must look at each other in the eye; they must make eye contact. Only then can you see the other person in their true light. – **CHAPTER 3**

It's difficult to realize that God is in control, but when we do, we have a better avenue to live out His will because deep down we always know that He wants what's best for us. During the moment this type of thinking can be challenging to say the least. People often say that patience is a virtue; what it is as well is a test—a test of your faith in God. – **CHAPTER 5**

Entrepreneurs who make a lot of money are so successful because they are able to think outside of the box. Thinking outside the box means the perimeter is going to bigger than simply thinking inside the box. It's a risk, and it ultimately takes more effort, but in the end, it's the only way to achieve success. When you think outside the box, and don't judge a book by its cover, paradoxically, you are able to within a person; you're able to see them for who they truly are. – **CHAPTER 7**

Beauty is found from within because our actions are ultimately the only thing we have control over. That's the gift of free-will.

The cross is the most important thing in Christianity, but once your sins are atoned for, God doesn't want you just to pray all day and sing and thank Him for it, he wants you to be a man after His own heart and spread the Gospel. He wants you to do all these things in response to that great gift you were given. – **CHAPTER 7**

It's interesting how unselfishness acts often pay dividends for us in the future; it's almost as if God sees where our heart is, appreciates it, and rewards us for our self-denial. – **CHAPTER 6**

In the same vein, it's an interesting point to wander why God made us in the first place. An answer you might normally get to that question is that He was lonely; but that isn't it. Since God is all powerful, omnipotent, and perfect, he doesn't *need* anything. It's the same choice married parents make when they decide to have children: they do so out of love—an unselfish love that transcends all understanding. Not only did our God come down from heaven to atone for our sins, but he also created us in the first place and allows us to have a relationship with Him. – **CHAPTER 6**

A day spent without encouraging others is a day wasted; people need you to be that agent of God in their life; there is no greater impact on your life than to impact others. – **CHAPTER 6**

Walking with God also means that you are willing to take a risk; sometimes that risk may involve you may look like a complete fool to others. If that's the case don't sweat it, for a fool to hu-

mans is often just the person God uses most to carry out His will.
– CHAPTER 4

It's interesting for me to look back on my own life and realize what has happened because certain things didn't happen. It reiterates to me that God had a plan for my life, and He knows not only how to shape it but direct it. **– CHAPTER 4**

When we hesitate, we are telling the thing or someone that we want that we don't want them—that they're not important in our life. When we have a chance to do God's will and don't act on it, we are telling Him that he is not the number one priority in our life. This disappoints God more than anything, because ultimately, he knows what's best for us. **– CHAPTER 4**

It was time to go into the world and see where I could leave my mark. My depression had ended now that I had finally seen some light, but what was I to do with my light? When you're an occasional runner, tying your shoes to go out and run is the hardest part; for me, it was time to tie my shoes. Learning how to tie one's shoes is something we learn how to do as a child, but the more and more we live, often times, the more and more we forget how to do this simple act. We're scared of what might happen if we fail; or, are we more afraid of what will happen if we succeed? Whatever it is, tying one's shoes is difficult, but with the Lord's help—and with His purpose in mind—we can do it each and every day. **– CHAPTER 4**

Compromising yourself is easy in times of trouble, but ultimately, there's always only one side that's right in disagreement, and that side is truth; to live the truth might mean sacrificing something, but in sacrificing that something, you'll find that you gain true honor and dignity—which could have never come without the sacrifice – **CHAPTER 3**

To start a relationship—whether it be romantic or simply friendship—there has to be a sense of permanence that will always be there. Without that, relationships cannot form properly—or at all. – **CHAPTER 6**

From The Pages of *After the Shampoo: Conditioned for Excellence*

Your parents are very important. They are literally the first people that condition your future behavior. – **CHAPTER 1**

The absolute worst thing that can happen in life is to be conditioned by someone who is good or great—incorrectly thinking in the back of your mind the whole time that they were excellent. – **CHAPTER 1**

When I think of the most ingrateful people in my life, I think of people who feel like they deserve everything. – **CHAPTER 1**

The most arrogant people I have met in my life aren't the ones who didn't brag about themselves, they are the ones who were unwilling to listen and unwilling to apologize. **– CHAPTER 2**

The most successful people in life leverage off other people's success instead of being jealous of them, knowing full well that the momentum of that other's success will lead to them their own success. **– CHAPTER 2**

Never let someone else's success become your own defeat. **– CHAPTER 2**

You see, the more attention we get in life, when that attention gets directed towards someone else, our first reaction is naturally to feel jealous. If this happens to you, don't beat yourself up about it, but you realize that you must turn that jealousy into encouragement. This way it's a win-win situation for both sides. **– CHAPTER 2**

In physics, a lever amplifies an input force to provide a greater output force, which is said to provide leverage. The ratio of the output force to the input force is the mechanical advantage of the lever. The mechanical advantage of a lever is the ratio of the load the lever overcomes and the effort a person or system applies to the lever to overcome some load or resistance. In simple words and as per the formula, it's the ratio of load and effort. Are you going to let the other person's success push you forward or push you back? **– CHAPTER 2**

How do you know if someone has made a big impact on this earth? The easiest way to see if this has happened is if someone says a person—who never said the quote in the first place—said that quote. – **CHAPTER 3**

There's a reason why people have misattributed these quotes to these people: they are more famous than the person who originally said it, thus making it more powerful of a quote. – **CHAPTER 3**

Throughout this book, I encourage you, the reader, to be conditioned by not good, not great, but excellent role models. I've got a question for you, though: how much more can you grow as person and in your walk with God if you can take the advice of people you don't like or don't respect? True, they might not have as good of as advice as the excellent, but you still might be able to grow from them. – **CHAPTER 3**

When giving advice, keep in mind that what you are about to propose to the other person is something new, something foreign. When you give someone a new food to try, you don't give them a whole spoonful, but only a bite. This is the way you should go about giving advice. – **CHAPTER 3**

The old can teach the young and the young can teach the old. – **CHAPTER 3**

All of us, no matter how successful we become, need encouragement. – **CHAPTER 3**

To condition someone, you must both challenge and encourage at an equal rate. When one gets in front of the other, excellence never happens. – **CHAPTER 3**

Oftentimes we cannot know God's ways; we can not see them. But, we have to always keep in mind that he can see us. It must be this way in order for Him to condition us, which in turn brings us along. **– CHAPTER 3**

As human beings, we are naturally conditioned to seek the approval of fellow man. All of us like to fit in, but at the same time, all of seek to be excellent. I've noticed that to be excellent, you have to sacrifice your incessant desire to fit in. **– CHAPTER 4**

As Williamson says, liberate yourself from your own fear. When you do so, others will follow suit. You will raise the bar for all. Excellence has a way of causing more excellence in the same way a virus spreads; it can truly be exponential. **– CHAPTER 4**

Dare to be the first one to do something; in doing so, you'll surprise many maybe even yourself. If you do something that has already been done before, the chances of you being remembered by ages to come go down significantly. If you're not consistently pushing yourself to be the first, you may as well not even attempt what you are doing, for it is in vain. **– CHAPTER 4**

When someone above you, with more experience and wisdom than you encourages you it is impossible to forget it; we're conditioned to not be taken seriously. **– CHAPTER 4**

Often times, when I think of my relationship with God, when he causes something to happen or not happen in my life, I realize that he has complete control of it—much more control of it then I have ... Because of this, he is able to bring me along. – **CHAP-TER 5**

To this day, the success I have had in writing, my technology sales career, and the education reform that I am working on currently, is due to the fact that I am not afraid to get people's opinion on matters. I'm constantly asking for advice; that's what my 6th book is about: being humble enough to seek advice. When you do this, you can become a subject matter expert on any topic even if you don't technically have a PhD in it. – **CHAPTER 5**

To become excellent, you must remember that if someone is critiquing you they think you are capable of something special— something to be remembered. Usually, when we don't hear criticism, we are happy; it I as if we did nothing wrong; I encourage us to do the opposite: we must seek out criticism in order to keep getting better. When you don't hear any, rather than be delighted, have the wherewithal to think that someone might not be taking you seriously. – **CHAPTER 5**

True, our present and future actions are dictated by our past actions, but at the same time, we have free will—we have the choice in which our destiny will be shaped. – **CHAPTER 5**

To be truly excellent, we must not be afraid to decline certain things, even if that thing be our very life. – **CHAPTER 5**

In order to influence, we must be influenced first. – **CHAPTER 5**

Dreaming is necessary when you're an underdog, and because you're forced to dream, versus knowing you'll achieve success all along, you're forced to outwork your competition, thus enabling to you achieve that long-awaited dream. People often forget this when analyzing the data on whether one will succeed or not. – **CHAPTER 5**

Like I said before, to achieve your dreams, you need someone to help condition you; you need someone to help bring you along. – **CHAPTER 5**

In the most meaningful relationships, each party must be humble enough to accept help from the other party. Without this, the type of learning and improved that is needed to become excellent can never happen. **– CHAPTER 6**

When you think outside the box, it not only levels the playing field for you an your competitors, it might even give you an edge to beat them. Because you're competition has more talent than you to begin with, they've never been forced to think outside the box; they've never been forced to be creative. If you remember this, you might just become like David and beat Goliath. **–** **CHAPTER 7**

As an underdog, if you already know what the person who is highly favored is going to do, use that to your advantage. As the cliché says, "knowledge is power." If you already know what there move is going to be, you have the power then to make your move. Battle is like chess; it's how you respond and react, can you be bold enough to make the right move? **– CHAPTER 7**

We must get outside of ourselves if we ever want to make anything of ourselves. When we look deeper into what I just said, we can discover the reason for this. A synonym for outside is exterior. When we think of the exterior of a peanut butter sandwich that is given to a child, he/she often doesn't want to eat the crust, but our parents growing up demanded that we finish our plate. One of the ten commandments from Exodus is "Honor your father and your mother, that your days may be long upon the land which the Lord your God is giving you." Ultimately, Jamal honors his mother and himself by go to the new school. When we honor our parents and "finish our plate," we can start to get outside and challenge ourselves more and more each and every day. – **CHAPTER 7**

CPSIA information can be obtained
at www.ICGtesting.com
Printed in the USA
LVHW010050150921
697830LV00010B/397

9 781954 617223